A Simpler Life

The School of Life

Published in 2022 by The School of Life
930 High Road, London, N12 9RT
First published in the USA in 2022

Designed and typeset by Ryan Bartaby
Printed in Latvia by Livonia Print

A proportion of this book has appeared online at
theschooloflife.com/thebookoflife

Every effort has been made to contact the copyright holders of the
materials reproduced in this book. If any have been inadvertently
overlooked, the publisher will be pleased to make restitution at the
earliest opportunity.

The School of Life is a resource for helping us understand ourselves,
for improving our relationships, our careers and our social lives – as
well as for helping us find calm and get more out of our leisure hours.
We do this through creating films, workshops, books, apps and gifts.

www.theschooloflife.com

ISBN 978-1-912891-68-9

10 9 8 7 6 5 4 3 2

A
Simpler
Life

A guide to greater serenity,
ease and clarity

Contents

Introduction   7

I. Simpler Relationships

i.   Becoming more straightforward   25
ii. Simpler dates   30
iii. Simpler relationships   35
iv. Simpler families   40

II. A Simpler Social Life

i.   What others think   49
ii. How many friends do we need?   60
iii. How often do we need to go out?   66

III. A Simpler Lifestyle

i.	How to live in a hut	75
ii.	How to enjoy a provincial life	89
iii.	Why we need quieter days	99
iv.	How to go to bed earlier	106
v.	How to be a modern monk	110
vi.	Good materialism	120

IV. Work and Simplicity

i.	Thinking rather than doing	137
ii.	Voluntary poverty	143
iii.	The terror of simplicity	151

V. Culture and Simplicity

i.	How to be less pretentious	159
ii.	How to read fewer books	164
iii.	How to care less about the news	172
iv.	How to travel less	178

Conclusion

i.	How to retire early	191
ii.	Glamour and simplicity	196
iii.	Purpose and simplicity	204

Introduction

Simplicity has become, for many of us, a word filled with longing and desire. We long to unburden ourselves of excess, to have more straightforward relationships, to declutter our homes and to avoid noise, complexity and fuss. Simplicity has grown central to our vision of happiness.

But it is notable – and revealing – that in historical terms, this yearning is very new. For most of our time on this planet, our aspirations have pointed in a radically different direction. Traditionally, whenever the chance arose, people's instincts ran towards enrichment and complexity; we wanted to embellish our environment, to demonstrate increasing sophistication and to live with greater opulence, formality, ritual and display.

A dramatic example of the movement away from this pattern of behaviour and towards a love of simplicity can be seen in the story of one particular clan.

Some time in the 1830s, a far from prosperous family moved into a very plain and modest farmhouse in New York state. They didn't select the house because they admired its rustic charms or because they were attracted to the stark angularity of its design. Their motivation was entirely pragmatic: it was affordable on their very limited budget. They lived simply not by choice but – as many people had always done – out of necessity.

It was in this house that, in 1839, the family's second child was born. He was named John Davison, and the family name was Rockefeller. This boy, known to most as J.D. Rockefeller, went on to make one of the greatest fortunes in economic history, founding in 1870 the Standard Oil Company, which at its peak held a near-monopoly on oil production in the USA. By his mid-fifties, Rockefeller had done what people throughout history had done when they had the opportunity: he bought land and set about building a triumphal mansion – a fabulously luxurious and ornate classical palace, with an imposing symmetrical façade topped by a stone statue of an eagle.

John Davidson's family home, Richford, New York State, USA

Kykuit, the J.D. Rockefeller Estate, Sleepy Hollow, New York State, USA, 1913

However, just a couple of generations later, when J.D.'s grandson (David Rockefeller, who now controlled much of the vast family fortune) built his own house, he went a very different way. David commissioned one of America's leading modernist architects, Philip Johnson, to build him a spartan minimalist base in Manhattan.

Philip Johnson, Rockefeller Guest House, Manhattan, USA, 1950

Though it sits on a very valuable piece of land, the exterior of the house is extremely restrained and its entrance almost humble. The internal spaces are white and unadorned: the concern throughout was for extreme serenity and simplicity.

David Rockefeller had every possible option open to him: he could have built something vast and swaggering, but what he really craved – like so many inhabitants of the modern world – was modesty and informality. Simplicity had stopped being a forced necessity to be escaped from at speed: it had become a philosophy to be aspired to.

Attributed to Antonio Rodriguez,
Portrait of Moctezuma II, 1680–1697

The same journey from complexity to simplicity can be traced in the development of a multitude of social and material trends, for example, in clothing. From the very beginning of recorded history, anyone of status and wealth tried to convey their position via the richness and splendour of what they wore.

No Aztec emperor would have dressed in clothes like those of his ordinary subjects; the uniform of a general was always more magnificent than that of a common soldier; a princess could never dress like a serving girl. But in modernity, there has been a radical shift. Today, those of great standing and power often opt for the simplest wardrobes.

Steve Jobs, former CEO of Apple Inc.

Similar transitions have taken place with our eating habits. As soon as our ancestors had the option, they devised separate dining rooms, where the eating of meals could be distanced from their preparation. If money was tight, the kitchen might be tiny and the dining room minute – but the separation was key. Only servants, farm labourers and factory workers ate in the kitchen. This trend continued for millennia. But in recent times, we've gladly chosen to return to the situation that earlier ages were desperate to flee.

The Sitting Woman and *The Thinker,* Hamangia culture, c. 5000 BCE

We see this in art, too. In 1956, a number of small clay statues dating from c. 5000 BCE were unearthed near the border between Romania and Bulgaria. Their faces and limbs are crudely modelled; there's no sign that the people who made them had the ability to reproduce the precise shape of a finger or of the muscles in a leg. The figures were simple *because that was all they could manage*.

Michelangelo, terracotta model for the *Pietà*, c. 1473–1496

Over succeeding millennia, sculptors went on to develop extraordinary technical capacities. In the late 15th century, Michelangelo produced a small-scale terracotta statue of Mary, the mother of Jesus, with her dead son lying across her lap, as a preparatory study for a much larger marble version known as the *Pietà*.

In the model, every limb is astonishingly accurate and the delicate modulation of bone, muscle and skin around each ankle or knee is perfectly rendered.

However, by the 1930s, the British sculptor Henry Moore had become famous for his crudely rendered figures, greeted as masterpieces by the prominent critics of the age.

Henry Moore, *Reclining Woman*, 1930

Technically, Moore was well able to reproduce the complex shapes of an elbow or a wrist. But he had chosen not to.

It was useful that the ancient clay figures from the Romanian–Bulgarian border were discovered in 1956 – when they could be recognised as powerfully expressive masterpieces – rather than in 1456 (or indeed 1856) when they would have been dismissed as bizarre curios, interesting only as evidence of the incapacity of primitive people to create genuine works of art. We rediscovered them just as our taste for simplicity could help us to perceive their beauty.

But why are we now so nostalgic for simplicity? Why has simplicity changed its place in our collective imagination? Why do we choose and esteem informal manners, plain or rustic objects and modest homes? In order to make sense of our enthusiasm, we can lean on a general theory of how taste is shaped.

First consider this portrait of Marie Antoinette, Queen of France, painted by Elisabeth Vigée Le Brun in 1778.

This painting, like so many other paintings of its era, is acutely interested in grandeur and status. The queen's hair, the hugely elaborate dress, the rich fabric draped over the table and the elegant flowers are all evocations of pre-eminence. But, ironically, security of position was what Marie Antoinette lacked – as did most people

Elisabeth Louise Vigée Le Brun,
Marie Antoinette in Court Dress, 1778

in her social circle. They were obsessed with displaying status because it could so easily be lost in the often violent and lawless state in which they lived – and so the painters of the day focused on representing the superiority that aristocrats were grasping for. This painting intimates the queen's intense need to assert her position in a fragile social hierarchy. Fifteen years after the painting was finished, France had broken out in revolutionary fervour – and Marie Antoinette made her way, alone, to the scaffold.

John Wayne's role was always the same: to represent what his audience thought was missing from their lives.

To consider another case of the compensatory dimension of taste, take Marion Michael Morrison, who became one of the most famous figures in the world during the middle decades of the 20th century – or at least he did under his stage name, John Wayne. Through a long series of immensely popular film roles, he came to represent a vision of tough self-reliance: his characters didn't bow to authority; they were impossible to intimidate; they never felt lonely, embarrassed or ashamed; they never worked in an office or had to get home to help with domestic chores. John Wayne's success didn't come from portraying the real lives of his audiences, but from embodying the independence and freedom they lacked – and yearned for.

From such examples, we can piece together a general thesis about taste: the taste of an era or a society reveals what people want more of but don't actually feel they securely possess. Earlier epochs didn't emphasise simplicity because there was no need to; a life with few possessions and plain food, early nights and plenty of time in the fresh air was available to everyone. But for us, simplicity plays the role that splendour once did for the aristocrats at Versailles or that rugged individualism did for the urban 20th-century accountants and dentists who watched John Wayne films. It is what we long for but don't have safely in our grasp.

Simplicity has become so elusive and desirable because the modern age is so troublingly, infinitely noisy and abundant. Industrialisation has made a vast array of products available to almost anyone at very low cost. We are bathed in options, surrounded by too much information with too many competing visions of happiness. We crave simplicity not because we are simple, but because we are drowning in complexity.

This book explores a set of ideas with the power to foster simpler lives. It considers the outer world – how we might build ourselves simpler living spaces, routines, working patterns and friendships – but it also looks at how we might achieve inner simplicity: how we might *feel* as straightforward as our pared down clothes or buildings *look*. The desire for a simpler life can too often be experienced as troubling and singular, but it is in reality a sane and widespread aspiration that we should listen to and honour. What follows is an undecorated and straightforward manual for the simpler life we hanker for – and deserve.

I.

Simpler Relationships

i. Becoming more straightforward

When discussing our aspirations for simplicity, there is something fundamental we should seek, long before we focus on simpler houses and clothes, simpler social lives and holidays: *simpler kinds of people.*

A 'simple person' is someone who speaks plainly about what they really want and who they really are. What makes simple people gratifying to be around isn't that their intentions are always unproblematic for us; it's that we know exactly what those intentions are from the start. Around simple, straightforward people, there is no need to second-guess, infer, decode, untangle, unscramble or translate. There are no sudden surprises. If they don't want to do something, they will, politely and in good time, explain that it's really not for them. If they're unhappy with our behaviour, they won't smile sweetly while developing noxious stores of envy or hatred in the recesses of their minds; they will immediately provide a gentle but accurate statement of how we are frustrating them. If they are worried a project is going awry, they won't pretend that all is well until a catastrophe can no longer be denied; they will speak up and try to fix the problem. If they are attracted to someone, they will find kind and inoffensive ways of making their feelings clear. And in bed, thcy may want to please, but they can also be honest and unashamed about what actually excites them.

People become frustratingly complicated when they doubt the legitimacy of their desires – and therefore don't dare to tell the world what they properly want and feel. They may appear to agree with everything we're saying, but it is likely to emerge that they have a host of reservations that will require an age to uncover and resolve. They will ask you if you'd like another slice of cake when they are pining for one themselves. They will swear that they want to join you for the dinner you suggested, when in reality they are aching for an early night. They will give every impression of being happy with you while crying inside. They will say sorry when they want you to apologise. They feel overlooked but won't ever push themselves forward or raise a complaint. They are longing to be understood but never speak. When they are attracted to someone, the only outward evidence might be a few sarcastic comments – which leaves the object of their affections bemused or unimpressed. And with sex, they go along with what they feel might be 'normal' as opposed to what actually interests them.

What could explain such confusing complexity? The root cause is poignant; it springs not from evil or cold manipulativeness, but from fear: the fear of how an audience might respond if one's true intentions were to be known.

There is, as is so often the case, likely to be a childhood origin to this pattern of behaviour. A child becomes complicated – that is, underhand, roundabout or even deceitful – when their earliest caregiver gives the impression that there is no room for honesty. Imagine a child whose needs (for another biscuit, for a run around the garden, for help with homework or for a chance not to see Granny) might have been received with obvious irritation or open anger. This child would never quite know when its parent would get annoyed or angry – or why. Or else the child might sense that a parent would be unbearably saddened if they revealed too many authentic aspirations. Why would any of us say how we feel or what we want, if the result were to be shouting and tears, or a complaint from a loved but fragile grown-up that this was a betrayal or all simply too much?

And so this child would grow expert at speaking in emotional code; would become someone who prefers always to imply rather than state, who planes the edge off every truth, who hedges their ideas, who gives up trying to say anything that the audience might not already want to hear; someone who lacks the courage to articulate their own convictions or to make a bid for the affection of another person.

Fortunately, none of us is fated to be eternally complicated. We can untangle ourselves by noticing and growing curious about the origins of our evasiveness and inadvertent slyness. We can register how little of our truth was originally acceptable to those who brought us into the world. Simultaneously, we can remind ourselves that our circumstances have changed. The dangers that gave birth to our coded manner of communicating have passed: no one is now going to shout at us, or feel inexplicably hurt, like they once did. Or if they do, we now have agency – we can, as a last but crucial resort, walk away. We can use the freedoms of adulthood to own up to more of who we actually are.

We can also recognise that our complicated behaviour doesn't please people as we might have hoped. Most of the people we deal with would far rather face frustration head on than be sold a fine tale and then have to suffer disappointment in gradual doses.

Human interaction always carries a risk of conflict: we are never far from misaligned goals and divergent desires. The simple and straightforward ones among us are lucky to have known enough love and acceptance early on in their lives to bear the danger of ruffling feathers; they invest their energies in trying to deliver their own truths with thoughtful diplomacy, rather than in clumsily burying them beneath temporary saccharine smiles. We discover the joys of simple communication when we can accept that what we want is almost never impossible for others to bear; it's the cover-up that maddens and pains.

ii. Simpler dates

One of the most powerful instincts we have when we meet someone we're attracted to is to try to please them, and we naturally assume that the best way to do this is to signal strongly just how much we agree with their views and choices on all matters great and small.

On an early date, when they happen to mention that they love dancing, we might reveal that, of course, we love dancing too. Or, when they explain how boring they find museums, we will hide the truth that on a trip to Berlin last year, we spent a whole, fascinating day in the galleries of the Altes Museum.

We may not state direct falsehoods, but we stretch and bend the truth to its limits, to create an impression of near-total alignment. Our will to please can reach a peak around sex: naturally, we can't possibly risk introducing another person to the unadulterated byways of our erotic imagination. Instead, we claim to want – by a miracle – exactly what they want.

It rarely occurs to us that they might be performing some of the same rigmarole for us; that they might also be adjusting their self-presentation in subtle ways to fit in with what they take to be our preferences and values. There's a tragicomic aspect to our deepening mutual attraction. Two decent people are trying to be as nice as they can. No one is setting out to deceive. And yet, gradually, a set of hugely misleading and dangerous ideas about who each person really is is being established.

The apparent success of our will to please can inspire us to move in together and later to marry. And then – inevitably – the prolonged, intimate scrutiny that coupledom brings reveals the scale of our mistaken expectations. In a sequence of disillusioning stages, we are each saddened, disappointed and shocked to discover who we have ended up with. There are recriminations, rows and fragile reconciliations until finally one or the other of us comes to the grim, but somehow still surprising, conclusion that we were never compatible.

Alternatively, we might stick at it, with growing misery. We may face a lifetime of holidays that never involve the museum visits we crave; resign ourselves to never having the kind of sex we want; or, even more grievously, eventually embark on a furtive life, seeking out the moments when the other is away to pursue the needs we've pretended not to have. Until, one day, our double life is exposed – and we drown in bitterness, fury and sorrow.

Sadly, the origin of such nightmares is only ever a touching, but risky and painfully flawed, devotion to being an easy match. We want to be simple, and yet we end up mired in a very complicated mess.

A genuinely simpler approach involves daring to be a bit more complex from the start. When the subject of dancing comes up, the sensible lover should immediately state their truth. When the museum theme is raised, they should declare their passion frankly. When it comes to their routines and tastes, they should mention the pleasure they take in (for example) a spotless kitchen worktop or explain what it means to them to be awake in the early hours, when the world is still sleeping and their mind is at its most adventurous.

There is no need to be brazen or demanding, just as there is no requirement that our date agrees or even sticks around beyond dessert (or the main course). Some will run away – and should. It will save everyone a great deal of time.

In order to be honest when seducing others, we need a basic acceptance of ourselves; we must know that we are not perfect but that we are not for that matter wholly abject or shameful. Our attitude to the kitchen might be a little excessive, but it is not delusional. Our very early rising might be unconventional, but it's perfectly sane – all things considered. We know that our sexual preferences might be statistically unusual, but they are not evil. An inner conviction that our oddities are essentially reasonable allows us to present ourselves to another person without fear or defensiveness.

This candour then arms us with the right to ask our date to reveal – with similar honesty – what may be individual and difficult about their own character. If they insist that they are really very simple and 'easy', we are allowed to be gently but firmly sceptical. They are a human being, and to be human is to be complicated. It cannot possibly be true that they exist without significant quirks.

Being straightforward on dates is a mechanism for two people to fast-forward time – and to spare themselves agony. We should know that a polished surface can't be a true picture of who anyone actually is. Only once our mutual complexities have been outlined should we believe that we are safe in the presence of a fellow mature and pleasingly direct individual. We will have the simpler relationships we desire when we can dare to share and accommodate the actual complexities of human nature.

iii. Simpler relationships

Many people, after they've been in a couple for some time, will privately admit that they are frustrated and disappointed by the person they've chosen to share their lives with.

If pressed for details, they will have no difficulty coming up with a list. They might complain that their partner:

· is too loyal to their irritating family

· doesn't share their views on the layout of the living room

· never wants to go on camping holidays

· plays tennis every Wednesday evening, no matter what

- doesn't like Moroccan food

- doesn't share their enthusiasm for 19th-century Russian novels

- has a friend who laughs for no apparent reason

- likes doing jigsaws

- has a habit of adding 'actually' to every second sentence, when it's actually redundant

As the list gets longer, they sigh; they still love their partner and long to be happy together, it's just that it seems impossibly complicated to make this relationship work.

What's driving their frustration isn't that they've fallen for an idiot as a mate; it's rather that we have all inherited needlessly complicated ideas of what a relationship is supposed to be. We are taught that love involves the almost total merging of two lives. We expect that a loving couple must live in the same house, eat the same meals together every night, share the same bed, go to sleep and get up at the same time, only ever have sex with (or even sexual thoughts about) each other, regularly see each other's families, have all their friends in common – and pretty much think the same thoughts on every topic at every moment.

It's a beautiful vision, but a hellish one, too – for it places an impossibly punitive burden of expectation on another human. We feel that our partner must be right for us in every way, and if they're not, they should be prodded and cajoled into reform.

But there is another perspective: relationships don't have to be so complicated and ambitious, if only we can keep in mind the things that, in the end, actually make them fulfilling. If we boil matters down, there might really be just three essential qualities we need from one another:

Kindness
A partner who is gentle with our imperfections and can good-humouredly tolerate us as we are.

Shared vulnerability
Someone with whom we can be open about our anxieties, worries and problems; someone we don't have to put on a front for; someone around whom we can be weak, vulnerable and honest – and who will be the same around us.

Understanding

Someone who is interested in, and can make sense of, the obscure features of our minds: our obsessions, preoccupations and ways of seeing the world. And whom we are excited to understand in turn.

If we have these three critical ingredients to hand, we will feel loved and essentially satisfied, whatever differences might later crop up. Perhaps our partner's friends or routines won't be a delight, but we will be content. Just as if we lack these emotional goods, and yet agree on every detail of European literature, interior design and social existence, we are still likely to feel lonely and bereft.

By limiting what we expect a relationship to be about, we can overcome the tyranny and bad temper that bedevils so many lovers. A simpler, yet very fulfilling, relationship could end up taking a more minimal form than one might expect: we might not socialise much together. We might hardly ever encounter each other's families. Our finances might overlap only at a few points. We could even live in different places and only meet up twice a week. Conceivably, we might not even ask too many questions about each other's sex life. But when we are together it will be profoundly gratifying because we will be in the presence of someone who knows how to be kind, vulnerable and understanding.

A bond between two people can be deep and important precisely because it is not played out across all practical details of existence. By simplifying – and clarifying – what a relationship is for, we release ourselves from overly complicated conflicts, and can focus on our urgent, underlying needs to be sympathised with, seen and understood.

iv. Simpler families

A few lucky ones among us get on easily with their parents, but for most of us, mothers and fathers are the source of continually complicated and emotionally draining trials. One strategy to simplify matters is to confront them. We may feel that we have said too little for too long and must – finally – get things off our chest. We will pick a moment and then explain how they hurt us and what they still misunderstand. We will lay out the ways in which their inadequacies took a toll on our childhood and continue to damage our chances today.

It is a moving ambition, but a highly risky one as well. Instead of meekly agreeing with our verdict, parents have a habit of turning around and, with surprising and humiliating authority, blaming us for being ungrateful and immature. Or we might decide to pull back at the final moment, sensing their vulnerability and inability to understand whatever we are trying to say, because it would be unbearable to inflict pain on them. Alternatively, they may seem to take it all on board, thank us for our candour and, at the very next encounter, express an opinion that makes it obvious that they have grasped nothing. After building up hope, it could feel as if the sane thing to do would be never to see these dangerous people again.

The situation is especially complex as, in most instances, the parent in question isn't an outright monster. They may be maddening in truly debilitating ways, but they can also be sweet or bright, funny or tender. We can't merely dismiss them as catastrophes. In the background, we likely have deep reserves of love for them: there's a favourite photo of them helping us build a sandcastle at the beach that brings tears to our eyes. We are moved by their familiar smells and routines. We hate them and, even more troublingly, care for them a lot. We want them dead and will be devastated when they are gone.

To simplify our relationships with our parents, it can help to depersonalise our ambivalence and pain. The exact reasons why we can't get on with our parents will be specific; the fact that we can't is extremely, and cathartically, general. Every parent brings a great deal of trouble into their child's life; every parent substantially harms and burdens the small person that they – in theory – wish simply to help. If they are unduly irritable (because of the terror and disappointment in their own background), the child will be cowed into timidity. If they are too gentle and indulgent, the child may fail to temper its own aggressive and egotistic tendencies. If the parent is (out of concern) overly controlling, the child will struggle to acquire an independent sense of direction. The possibilities for error are infinite. Naturally, we resent the unique mistakes our own early caregivers inflict on us, but we are participating in a more or less universal fate. It's not really our parents who were the problem; it is that infants have no option but to allow their minds to be shaped by the random set of average, and consequently flawed, adults in their vicinity.

Moreover, because parents are a generation older, much of what shaped them stemmed from a world with priorities, values, anxieties and hopes that seem strange – even reprehensible – to their children, but that were, and still are, urgent and real for them. Given where they came from, perhaps it isn't a surprise that they care so much about money or status, manners or education – and so little about honesty and trust, warmth and calm. When we have our own children, we can be sure that they'll feel the same boredom, resentment and bafflement we currently do, in response to attitudes that we haven't even thought to notice or rein in.

It's perhaps unsurprising that our parents retain a vision, as irksome as it is constant, of us as children. They remember how long it took for us to mature. Our first tumbling steps and our earliest attempts to string a few words together are for them still vivid, and perhaps deeply fond, memories. At some level, it's almost understandable if they are condescendingly amazed that we have a job or can drive a car and doubt whether we should ever really be allowed to make our own choices about whom to marry or where to live.

Simplicity in our familial relationships must spring from a recognition of the inherent complexity of what we're trying to do – which is to get on well with someone who has unavoidably damaged us and whose outlook on life can never reasonably align with our own.

Resignation can sound bleak, but with it comes hope – limited, but mature. In a simpler relationship, we anticipate that certain occasions are bound to be difficult, and in doing so help them to be slightly less so. If we spend a holiday with our parents, we know that they will – within minutes – put their finger on our most vulnerable dimensions. If we have lunch with them, we know they'll steer the conversation to our ineptitude (as they see it) in money or love. These occasions will no longer be dreaded because we will have already forced ourselves to consider their troublesome aspects as understandable and beyond our control.

In a simpler relationship with our parents, we don't keep trying to get from them the things that they have shown themselves unable to offer. We know that they will never understand our childhood sorrows or why we have chosen our partner, so we don't launch into futile attempts at explanation. Instead, we focus, as much as possible, on the few areas where we can be peaceable together. We might remember that they like talking about their friends, so we can ask them many open-ended questions about their visits and chats. If they are keen on gardening, we can draw them out on their tomato plants or the impact of some recent heavy rain showers.

In this new, simpler way of dealing with our parents we can be strategic about where, and for how long, we see them. If they have a tendency to grow fussy and snobbish in restaurants, suggest a walk in the country. If we like their taste in kitchen utensils, fix up a trip to a department store to get their advice about a new breadboard. We can decide never to stay overnight with them. With a clear sense of all that could go wrong, we are free to focus our attention on the few things that might reliably deliver satisfaction.

A parent and an adult child are emotionally intertwined, in intricate ways, for reasons that have nothing to do with personal preference. We're tied by history and biology to a being who was a god-like giant when we were tiny, but whose flaws we have since come to know in great and very painful detail. This never happens outside families: in no other situation are we forced into a death-bound union with someone who – given our divergent temperaments, tastes, habits and attitudes – we would never dream of selecting as a friend. We would do well to accept that as a strange, yet constant and simple, feature of the human condition, we are all emotionally tethered for life to someone who is both an irritating stranger with maddening habits and the person who wept for joy when we were born.

A Simpler
Social Life

i. What others think

There is one thing that makes our lives a great deal more complicated than they should be: that is, that we are rarely far from the oppressive worry of 'what other people think'. Inside the courtrooms of our minds, we are continually weighing up the legitimacy of our wishes and thoughts in relation to the imagined verdicts of numerous, nebulous 'others'.

It's an understandable concern. In evolutionary terms, we are the descendants of people who, for thousands of generations, survived by keeping on the right side of their foraging tribes. Diverging from established rituals or customs, refusing to accept the hierarchy or just being thought odd could lead to isolation, exclusion and, ultimately, death. Caring about the thoughts of others was a critical adaptive advantage.

However, this social pressure is just as prevalent in individual upbringings today. The powerful role played by our parents, our peers and our schools means that by the time we reach adulthood, we are likely to have absorbed and taken to heart a significant set of collective precepts about everything from what counts as success or failure, who is admirable and who deserves to be reviled, to what it means to be educated and to have a 'nice' home, what constitutes a proper career and what kinds of love life are decent.

As a result of this forceful – but covert – education, we toe a narrow and cautious line. We might back away from an intriguing professional option because our mother and her friends would strongly disapprove. Or we might stick with a job that doesn't utilise the most interesting parts of who we are because the people we were at college with see it as prestigious. We may officially be free to follow our intimate preferences, but in reality we're subject to disguised pressures to conform to previously received scripts.

In search of a simpler and more singular existence, what strategies might usefully liberate us from this excessive deference to the judgements of others? We can identify three main mechanisms for reducing the burden of groupthink.

1. An aristocratic view

The word 'aristocratic' tends to evoke visions of people with top hats, castles and an ancient lineage, but in its pure form, it refers to something very different and far more useful: someone who follows their own mind, who reasons independently and who is instinctively suspicious of popular assumptions. Our loyalty to democracy is unfortunately seldom limited to the very sensible belief that leaders should be elected by a fair ballot of all the citizenry. Instead, problematically, our democratic instincts show up in a strong tendency to assume that the broad consensus of our society must invariably be correct on all matters – from how much money we should have to how to raise a child. On the contrary, an aristocrat of the mind assumes that the mass consensus could very well be wrong in many instances. It's not arrogance or conceit that motivates this attitude; it comes, instead, from an unflinching recognition of some of the basic flaws in collective thinking.

For one thing, society's assumptions are only ever broad generalisations: they are, at best, statements about what most people happen to like or dislike. Opinion polls can at times be quite accurate generalisations – but that doesn't say anything about how relevant they are to our own, specific cases. The Louvre in Paris is, by common agreement, one of the most interesting museums in the world, and it is taken to be a must-see attraction when one is visiting the city. But a more aristocratically minded traveller (who could be staying in a youth hostel, perhaps) might well opt to skip the place entirely and instead spend their time investigating the rubbish collection system of the capital – because this happens to be where their authentic interests lie.

We're generally good at recognising the limitations of group wisdom when it clashes with avowed expertise: we don't think that an eye surgeon should base their treatments on 'what most people think'. But we don't similarly embrace the idea that we can be experts on ourselves and our own needs. A revered novel won't have received its accolades based on a close examination of our personal ideal reading matter, but rather on what a lot of people happen to find impressive – and yet we tend to immediately imagine that it must be something we should enjoy and must read soon. The genuinely aristocratic approach isn't to disdain the opinions of others, but to see these for what they are: statements about what many people think is important, which have no special authority when it comes to working out what we, as individuals, should feel or do next.

The aristocratically minded person has a good sense of history. They are aware of how consensus changes, quite dramatically, over time. Ideas from forty years ago about marriage or work, politics or sexuality now often strike us as quaint or absurd. The aristocrat draws the lesson that today's 'obvious' truths are equally fragile, and they therefore don't feel they owe them any special respect or adherence.

The aristocrat is also struck by an odd feature in the shaping of consensus. It needn't genuinely be the case that everyone agrees with a leading idea. What often powers the appearance of unanimity is the (erroneous) assumption each person has that everyone else is convinced of something. For example, person A has doubts about an idea but keeps them under wraps because they imagine that person B is rock solid in their conviction – but in fact, person B has their own doubts as well and, in turn, they keep quiet about them because person A seems to be a staunch supporter. The aristocrat is alive to the dark comedy inherent in the psychology of consensus.

We don't need a landed estate to qualify as an aristocrat; what counts is the very sane conviction that 'what most people think' isn't and should never be a reasonable guide to our own lives.

2. Loving ourselves more

The second mechanism for caring less about what others think is to love ourselves a little more. We tend to crave the validation of others and to care about how they see us in inverse proportion to how well we think of ourselves. If we – independent of others – trusted that we were decent and good, we'd not be so affected by the level of esteem accorded to us by others. But for a range of unfair, yet seemingly compelling, reasons we tend to think very badly of our own natures.

For a start, we know every facet of our own laziness, confusion and error. We are experts in the many ways in which we've let other people down, bungled our chances and done foolish things, but we have no comparable information on the lives of others (who tend carefully to edit out their flaws from public view). Naturally, we then assume that we are weirder, and less worthy, than others and in turn seek out – and worry about losing – the good opinion of strangers who appear to share in none of our idiocies. But, of course, we are being too kind to others – and too harsh on our own characters. We mustn't compare our inner reality with the deceptive façades of those around us.

We deserve to accord ourselves a little of the attitude that a good parent has towards their offspring. This kind of parent is legendary for the loyalty they show when their child is in difficulty. The whole world may be jeering, but the parent stays firm: they can find it in themselves not to be punitive about whatever the divorce, sexual scandal, criminal proceedings or plagiarism accusations may be. When everyone else is mocking, the parent will show up at their child's side – or even the prison gates – every day. This kind of behaviour might be read as a biological anomaly that tells us nothing about the actual merits of the offspring in question, but there is something deeper and more interesting going on. The parent stays on the child's side for one central reason: they understand them fully.

They know that, from the outside, the child could be dismissed as a 'felon', 'an idiot' or 'disgusting'. But no human is ever simply their worst moment – and every worst moment has a long history, which invariably merits a high degree of sympathy. The more we know of someone, the more difficult it becomes to caricature them with a single hostile slogan. Hatred is just a result of standing too far away, not daring to investigate who a person might really be or what they have gone through. There are – in the end – very few monsters; there are mostly only hasty judgements.

It is because the parent stands so near to their child – because they were there from the child's first moment and have seen their struggles and know their history – that they will be natively inclined to extend complex compassion to them. What might look like foolishness, greed, degeneracy or sickness from afar emerges, through a nuanced, fine-grained knowledge of the whole story, as something very different. We could weep for anyone if we really knew what they had gone through. The parent loves their child because they understand them. Parents are, for good reason, the least consensus-driven people in the world. No wonder they wait at the prison gates.

Though rarely spoken of, this way of thinking provides us with a model for an elevated way of looking at ourselves and of considering our errors. It is an alternative to shame and lifelong self-hatred. When we are too hard on ourselves, and doubt our worth or right to exist, it is because we haven't fully observed and remembered how hard it is, through no particular fault of our own, to be us. We may feel we have failed to make the most of our lives, but it is not (as we are punitively inclined to think) because we are leaden-souled wasters or reprobates, but because we came from a very difficult place and have had many demons to wrestle with. Like the ideal loving parent, we should keep the past firmly in mind and feel sorrow and sympathy for the problems it has generated; and like the ideal loving parent, we should insist that, despite everything, we are precious and worth keeping faith with.

If we are able to foster a parental perspective on ourselves, irrespective of what the rest of the world happens to think, we can legitimately (and without falling into narcissistic exaggeration), see ourselves as honourable and worthy of regard – despite everything. And if we can feel a proper, deserved compassion for ourselves, our interest in how others may judge us recedes: in the end, it doesn't matter if they respect or love us; we love and respect ourselves enough to endure.

3. Trusting our own experience

The third mechanism for caring less about what others think is to trust our own experience a little more. It might sound odd, and frankly a little insulting, to suggest that we may not know if we're enjoying ourselves or what our real thoughts and desires are, but for much of our lives we've been conditioned to align our inner responses with socially established conclusions – to the extent that we may have almost entirely lost touch with our authentic perspectives.

If we read a distinguished review informing us that one particular café is the best in town, we may instinctively feel we are having a good time when we are there. If we are told a certain film is a masterpiece, we tend automatically to feel impressed by what we are seeing. Out of respect for the judgements of others, we may tune out the faint – but always audible – signals that our own minds are sending us.

In this respect, we should remember to be more child-like. As children don't know what they are supposed to think, they naturally go with their true feelings – and sometimes come out with startlingly insightful and prescient judgements as a result. Trusting their own minds, they tell us that Granny is a bit selfish or that spiders are pretty; they blurt out that a lavish wedding was very boring or that the nicest thing in the world is to lie on the floor looking at the ceiling.

Once we throw off the shackles of what other people think, and how we assume we're meant to feel, we're free to discover what genuinely matters to us, however eccentric or odd it might appear. We can discover for ourselves what manner of life pleases us, and the fact that it may look absurd or ridiculous or frivolous to others won't particularly bother us. We're not setting out with a desire to shock or offend – for to want to shock is still to be focused on what others think. Yes, it would be nice to have the approval of our peers, but if we can't get it, we can carry on with modest indifference. They might have the numbers, but it's our life, and it's not to be wasted living by values that are not true to our own insights and happiness.

With such freedom of mind, it becomes far easier to lead what we wanted all along: a simpler life.

ii. How many friends do we need?

In the modern world, we are expected to have a lot of friends. A busy social life is looked upon as a primary marker of success. It feels absolutely necessary to go out at least once every weekend (see page 66), to have a substantial crowd at our wedding and for our funeral to be a rather busy affair.

But when searching for greater simplicity and calm, we need to ask an unfamiliar question: *what are friends for?* This is not cynical – there's no suggestion that friendship has no purpose at all – we are just quietly and honestly asking what it is that we ideally want from spending time with other people.

If we don't really know what friends are for, we can't tell how many we need. It's a general truth: the more we know what we're trying to achieve in any area, the simpler and plainer our lives can become. To make an analogy: suppose we set off to collect sticks in the forest. We could pick up lots of them – but how many do we actually need? The answer depends on what we need them for: lighting a fire to cook supper, or making a shelter for the night? It's only a sense of purpose that allows us to see how much of anything is enough. It is in this spirit that we can ask what we are looking for from friends.

1. They broaden our sense of normality

Left to our own devices, we often come to the painful conclusion that we are among the strangest people alive. We're acutely aware of the bizarre impulses of our own imaginations, the regrettable things we've done at 3 a.m., our stabs of resentment against those who have been kind to us, how we farted in the lift coming up to the office, our fiendish strategies for procrastination and the occasional longing to abandon every responsibility and fling ourselves out of the nearest window. Unfortunately, all we have to compare ourselves with, most of the time, is the polished surface of the people we meet day to day, going placidly about their business, seemingly free from all the weirdness we know exists in ourselves. A good friend is kind enough to hear our tentative revelations without surprise or shock – and with a wry look of recognition. They are willing to let us in on the odd dimensions of what it is like to be them, so that we can see how universal eccentricity always is; they don't necessarily have the same private madnesses as we do, but they intimately understand the problems that come from being alive and are ready to share details with us with candour and good humour. Again and again, good friends can provide us with the evidence we lacked about our own fundamental normality. Through their warm, sympathetic, knowing reception of our confessions, and their equal admissions, they help us to reframe our sense of what being 'normal' really means. They pierce our loneliness and save our sanity. No wonder we feel close to them.

2. They help us be less vague

One of the most basic characteristics of the human mind is its powerful tendency to be vague. In so many areas, we know only roughly what we think: what do we really feel about a new relationship, what kind of job suits us or what is truly causing us to be so anxious and irritable? The truth lies somewhere in our minds, but we're usually unable to bring it into focus by ourselves, however long we spend thinking about our dilemmas. This is where a friend comes in. The person who first realised this was the ancient Greek thinker and founding figure of Western philosophy, Socrates, who argued that conversation with friends was the ideal medium in which to straighten out our thoughts – and gain insight in a way that we never could when by ourselves. A good friend will sort through our rambling or confused statements and bring their intelligence to bear on topics that we are too frightened or ashamed of to investigate properly. We can tell them that we can't decide what to do after our studies, or what part of town to get an apartment in, or why our mother makes us sad, and they can render us one of the kindest services anyone can offer: to sit with us for an hour or two – perhaps with a pen and paper – and sort through the emotions and options with us, untying the knots in our solitary ideas. They can help us to know ourselves better than we could on our own.

3. They ease us out of our defensive postures

Our intimate histories have shaped all of us in slightly unfortunate ways. A scary and powerful parent might have left us with an exaggerated respect for authority, but it's not something we can easily recognise about ourselves. Alternatively, perhaps our early years around a fragile parent have made us deeply anxious about inadvertently upsetting others, and so rendered us too prone to inner contortions to avoid conflict. Because these ways of interacting are so familiar to the person who experiences them, we may not easily be able to see where we are making errors. We become dispirited, hemmed in, worn down, inhibited, repressed – and don't know why. However, a good friend has an eye for our emotional creases, as well as the kindness and patience to draw our attention to them in a way that we can absorb and that won't humiliate us. They point us towards the unwittingly retained defensive or shamed postures we acquired out of necessity long ago, but which no longer serve our best interests. Others might notice that we're oddly timid or too keen always to be right, but very few care enough about us to bring this to our notice in a way we can bear. A true friend is sympathetically curious about how we've come to be as we are; they are deeply attentive to the story of our background – and they want to be of service. Most importantly, they are sufficiently generous and kind to accompany us on our stumbling, imperfect path to maturity.

*   *   *

None of these three psychological needs puts any boundaries on what else we might do with a genuine friend: we could be buying each other cocktails at a bar or roping ourselves together for a final assault on the summit of K2. But if we peer beneath the surface activity – look past the bowl of olives, the special glasses or the crampons and safety harnesses – what makes certain friendships satisfying is that, along the way, one or more of our core needs is being met.

We might be exceptionally lucky and find all three essential qualities of friendship in one person. Or we might be fortunate in another way and discover more than one individual capable of helping us. But what we discover is that the core answer to the question 'How many friends do we need?' tends to be: 'Far fewer than we normally suppose – so long as they are delivering the true satisfactions of friendship.'

Once we have a clearer sense of what we're looking for in our social life, we can, with relief, politely back out of so many of our less fruitful acquaintanceships and concentrate our affection and interest on the very small number of people who properly honour the core functions of friendship. We should feel extremely lucky if we manage to lay claim to three friends worthy of the title in a lifetime.

iii. How often do we need to go out?

One of the major reasons why our lives are so busy is that we come under immense pressure to 'go out' – usually in the evening, and typically to one of the most peculiar and paradoxical of all human social inventions: parties.

It is because these parties are so ubiquitous and benefit from such widespread approval that we're liable to miss how confusing and unhelpful they can be to our sensitive inner selves.

What draws us to leave home and attend a party or social gathering isn't merely a sense of duty; it is the desire to connect deeply with other humans, to attenuate a perhaps painful sense of isolation and to find an echo of our fears and longings in the eyes of others.

However, the events that typically take place when we reach the party should lead us to interrogate the pressures we are under to leave home. On arrival, it is usually evident that the hosts have been to a lot of trouble: their place may look spotless, glasses may be sparkling on a side table and the room will perhaps be crowded with a lot of well-turned-out individuals enjoying energetic conversations.

But if we were to conduct an anthropological investigation into what was actually being said, we would likely discover that the guests, rather than conversing freely, are acting in accordance with a well-established and rigid social code that could lead us to doubt why we would ever freely opt to leave our house, travel across town and stand in the centre of a room holding a glass and wondering who to talk to next. Eight rules for this socially entrenched party code come to mind:

1. Emphasise your successes, though boast only covertly.

2. Never allude to troubles, doubts or worries; apparently no one comes to a party to hear what is going on in another's heart.

3. As much as possible, agree with others. If someone is talking about their new puppy, say, 'How lovely' – especially if you dislike dogs. If someone mentions that they've been on a skiing holiday at the foot of a mountain you've never heard of, remark, 'Oh, that's amazing.'

4. Keep it light: laugh, even if you don't especially find anything funny. Look for the amusing side of every topic.

5. Don't reveal any earnest aspiration to connect with a fellow broken and ailing human.

6. Mingle: it's rude to talk at length with anyone; speak to as many people as possible, even if only for a minute.

7. Hug people you would normally cross the road to avoid.

8. If anyone fails to stick to the rules and says or does something 'wrong' (like being sincere), slip off rapidly to talk to someone else who knows how to behave 'properly'.

It's tantalising. All of us have rich and complex histories. All of us have dazzling minds that can record the most subtle impressions and are filled with tender and poignant scenes accumulated over decades. We all had complicated childhoods, are ambivalent about our careers, troubled by despair and anxiety, worried about our relationships, puzzled by sex – and heading towards decay and death far sooner than we can bear. And yet still we continue to remark on the traffic and ask about each other's recent holidays.

How many sincere revelations might we discover in our new companions if only we could: what happened in their childhoods, how they found their way through adolescence, what they make of their parents, what they dislike about themselves, what makes them fall into bed sobbing, whether they have ever thought of suicide. Sadly, the codes governing our social interactions ensure that we will never come close to any such enquiries. We may have been asked along to the evening, but our deeper selves have not been invited.

The moral is clear. If we seek others, we should stay at home; if we wish to alleviate loneliness, we should turn down invitations; if we want company, we would be better off communing with dead writers and poets than hunting for solace at large gatherings.

We must cease to be ashamed of our buried longings to remain by ourselves. It is very normal, and highly understandable, for properly social people – that is, people who really wish their souls to connect with those of others – to feel anxious about parties, and to prefer to see people very seldom and then only in the smallest and most intimate of contexts. If we really crave the love and understanding of other people, it is too much to bear the humiliations and betrayals involved in the average get-together. We should restrict our social lives to the occasional, exceptional evening out with a true friend who can both laugh and cry with us, sympathise with us and exchange authentic and heartfelt notes with us on the fleeting ecstasies and long-running sorrows of being human. That will be a 'party' worth breaking our isolation for.

A Simpler
Lifestyle

i. How to live in a hut

There's a dread that we normally keep at the far edges of our minds but which occasionally – particularly at 3 a.m. on a restless night – floods our thoughts. It is that if we don't constantly strive to achieve – if we slip up, or if some new catastrophe strikes the economy – we'll lose pretty much everything and we'll end up living in a caravan, a tiny one-room flat or – God forbid – a hut in the middle of nowhere.

The bleakness of this image of destitution – whatever form it may take for you – spurs us on to ever more frantic efforts. We'll settle for almost anything to avoid it: oppressively long working hours, a job that holds no interest, risky money-making schemes, a loveless marriage that keeps us in the family home or, perhaps, decades suffering the whims of a grim relative in the prospect of an inheritance. The hut is a symbol of disaster and humiliation.

It's in this fear-laden context that we might consider the case of a man called Kamo no Chōmei, who was born in Japan in around 1155. His father was the well-to-do head of a prominent religious shrine near Kyoto, which was then the capital, and Chōmei grew up in luxurious circumstances. He received a refined education and in the early part of his adult life had an elegant social circle. When he was still in his twenties, his grandmother left him a large house and his future looked bright. But then it all started to go wrong. He made enemies and was sidelined in his career; he got into financial difficulties and, by the time he was fifty, he had alienated his former friends, had practically no money left – and was going bald.

Chōmei was forced to reform his lifestyle and exist on the most slender material means. He built himself a tiny hut far out in the country, where no one else wanted to live – just 3 metres (or 10 feet) square. It was, he reflected, one-hundredth of the size of the mansion in which he'd grown up. It wasn't even a permanent structure; his situation was so precarious that he had to ensure his home could be dismantled and carted away.

A modern reconstruction of the hut shows just how small and basic it was – but doesn't convey its isolated

Reconstruction of Kamo no Chōmei's hut
within the Kawai-jinja Shrine, Kyoto, Japan

position in the hills near Toyama, an area that was
considered the back of beyond. Rotting leaves collected
on the roof; moss grew on the floor; the water supply
was just a rickety bamboo pipe leading from a nearby
stream to a little pool by the door. Chōmei cooked
outside, eventually rigging up a small awning to keep
the rain off in wet weather. He slept on a pile of bracken
on the floor, had no furniture and lived mainly on nuts,
berries and wild root vegetables, which he foraged from
the woods – though quite often he went hungry. The
only people he saw were a peasant family who lived at
the foot of the hill and who his former grand friends
would have dismissed as lowly rustics. He could only

afford clothes made from the coarsest cloth and they soon became mere rags, leaving him indistinguishable from the beggars he used to see in the city. It was here, in this way, that Chōmei lived for fifteen years, until his death in his mid-sixties.

It was also here that he wrote a short book, *The Ten Foot Square Hut* – one of the great masterpieces of Japanese literature. It's not – as we might expect – a lament, poring over the misfortunes and betrayals that led him to this degraded condition. Instead, it's full of good cheer, happiness and pleasure; one of the most touching lines is the simple affirmation: 'I love my little hut, my simple dwelling.'

What was it that enabled Chōmei to find fulfilment in such an apparently unpromising place? It wasn't that he was naturally drawn to a minimal material life: no one who'd known him earlier, in his days of prosperity, would have imagined that he would thrive under such circumstances – least of all himself. He wasn't someone who for years had been hankering for the simple life. He moved to the hut in desperation and against his inclinations; it was only once he was there that he discovered that he liked it – that it was, in fact, his ideal home.

Chōmei was guided by a distinctive philosophy. For us to follow this is a principle of hope, for we can't magically take on another individual's personality – but we can understand, and perhaps come to share, their ideas. Temperament may be fixed, but philosophy is transferable. From his book, we can identify four crucial ideas that together transformed what could have been an utterly grim experience into one of deep and tranquil satisfaction.

1. Beauty is very important

It seems like a strange place to start. Normally, one would imagine beauty to be the outcome of immense wealth: elegant possessions, a gracious home and trips to Venice and St Petersburg. But these expensive things are just the most obvious examples of beauty. As our taste becomes more sensitive and our imagination more expansive, the link with monetary wealth falls away – because many truly lovely sights are readily available to those who know how to look.

Around his modest home, Chōmei – with a sensitive eye – discovered endless sources of beauty: autumn leaves, fruit trees in blossom, melting snow, the sound of the wind rustling through the trees and the rain beating down on the roof. All were free. He was entranced by flowers: 'In spring I gaze upon swathes of wisteria, which hang shining in the west like the purple clouds that bear the soul to heaven.' He found a delightful spot on the hillside: 'If the day is fine ... [I] look out over Mount Kohata, Fushimi Village, Toba and Hatsukashi,' and at night 'the fireflies in the nearby grass blend their little lights with the fishermen's fires of distant Makinsohima.'

The idea of having to cope with constant ugliness is part of what makes a lower-level economic life so frightening. Chōmei's antidote is to stress the continuing opportunities for visual delight, even on the most minimal of incomes.

2. Time is more important than money

Although we say that time is precious, our actions reveal our real priorities: we devote a huge portion of our conscious existence to making, and trying to accumulate, money. We have a detailed and definite sense of financial accounting, while time invisibly slips away.

Chōmei, on the contrary, had a keen sense of the value of his own time, without interruptions, impediments or duties: 'I can choose to rest and laze as I wish, there is no one to stand in my way or to shame me,' he remarks.

He had time to practice playing the *biwa* (lute): 'My skills are poor,' he admits, but he had no audience and wasn't trying to please or impress anyone: 'I play alone, I sing alone, simply for my own fulfilment.' He read and reread the same few favourite books, which he came to know almost by heart; he had time to reflect and to write; he meditated, took long walks and spent a lot of time contemplating the moon.

Chomei's activities were self-directed: he did them simply because he found them enjoyable, not because anyone had asked him to do them or because they were expected of a civilised individual. And he had this luxury only because he had disregarded the nexus of money, and the pursuit of status that is so closely connected to it. Theoretically, Chōmei could have found a job, however lowly. But he preferred to cut down his expenses to zero in the name of something truly valuable: his time.

3. Everything is transient

Chōmei opens his book with a metaphor comparing human life to a river:

'On flows the river ceaselessly, nor does the water ever stay the same. The bubbles that float upon its pools now disappear, now form anew, but never endure long. And so it is with people in this world, and with their dwellings.'

With this, he is reminding himself – and us – of the half-terrifying, half-consoling fact that our existence, and all our pleasures and troubles, are fleeting.

Our lives are brief, and so it is the quality of our experiences, rather than the extent of our possessions, that matters. The more things we own, the more we are exposed to misfortune: a fashionable home will soon be outdated, our prestige in the eyes of others will fluctuate for trivial reasons and the monuments we hope to be remembered by will be misinterpreted or torn down. The hut is an impermanent accommodation – it might be blown down in a storm or washed away in a flood, officials might arrive at our door and force us to leave – but by living here our needs become so simple that chance has less to work on.

4. 'Worldly' people are less happy than they seem

One fear that erodes our willingness to live a simpler life – in a hut, if need be – is the haunting thought that other people are having a wonderful time while we are not. Perhaps we could manage to get by, but surely we'd always be conscious of how much we were missing out on.

Chōmei continually reminded himself that a 'worldly' life – which in his early and middle years he knew intimately – carries a heavy load of limitations, defects and sorrows. The life of the well-to-do is less enviable than it outwardly seems. The fashionable world is full of what he called 'cringing': 'You worry over your least action; you cannot be authentic in your grief or your joy,' he wrote. In high society, it is always paramount to consider how any opinion will be judged by the other members of the social beehive; envy is widespread and there is a perpetual anxiety of losing status – which takes the satisfaction out of prosperity: 'Without a peaceful mind, palaces and fine houses mean nothing.'

Chōmei's aim wasn't to disparage the rich. 'I am simply comparing my past life with my present one,' he wrote, adding that the balance of pleasures and contentment was distinctly in favour of the latter. What he had been denied wasn't – on examination – worth regretting.

*   *   *

Chōmei is just one hut dweller, but there have been many. The ancient Greek philosopher Diogenes (c. 400–323 BCE) lived for years in a barrel (sometimes taken to be a very large ceramic pot) in the marketplace of the wealthy city of Corinth. On one occasion he was visited by the emperor, Alexander the Great. Alexander approached with his retinue and asked if Diogenes wanted or needed anything. 'Yes,' replied the philosopher, 'could you move a little to the side? You are blocking the sunlight.' Many onlookers mocked him for missing this opportunity for riches, but the emperor reportedly remarked: 'Truly, if I were not Alexander, I wish I could have been Diogenes.'

Thomas Christian Wink, *Diogenes and Alexander*, 1782

More recently, in 1845, the American writer Henry David Thoreau – then 27 years old, a graduate of Harvard University and heir to a prosperous pencil manufacturing business – moved into a wooden cabin by the side of a small lake in Massachusetts, where he would spend the next two years. It was marginally bigger than Chōmei's modest home, as well as being more stoutly constructed and better equipped (having the luxuries of a fireplace and a writing desk), but the moral Thoreau drew was almost identical: to those who are inwardly free, there are riches enough available in a hut.

Interior of Thoreau's cabin, Walden Pond, Massachusetts, USA

Similar stories abound elsewhere in history. In 1881, German philosopher Friedrich Nietzsche spent the summer months living in a single, small rented room in a house in the Engadin Valley in Switzerland. He saw almost no one, went for long walks in the mountains and stuck to a plain diet. Though a far from hideous existence, it was much more basic than the standard of accommodation that, at the time, a distinguished professor – which Nietzsche had been up to this point – would have been expected to enjoy. But he adored it – and he came back for several months almost every year for the rest of the decade.

Nietzsche's room in Engadin, Switzerland,
where he lived on and off for several years

In the winter of 1913–1914, another philosopher, Ludwig Wittgenstein (who at the time was an extremely wealthy 24-year-old), designed and had built for himself a small wooden cabin on an isolated hillside overlooking a fjord in Norway.

Wittgenstein's remote residence, Skjolden, Norway

He was to spend much of his time there over the next two decades, until the deteriorating political condition of Europe made it impossible. In 1936, he wrote to a friend: 'I do believe that it was the right thing for me to come here, thank God. I can't imagine that I could have worked anywhere as I do here. It's the quiet and, perhaps, the wonderful scenery; I mean, its quiet seriousness.'

What these cabin- and hut-dwelling people have to teach us isn't that we should actually live in miniscule cabins or single small rooms. Rather, they are showing us that it's *possible* to live in materially minimal conditions, while being good-humoured, ambitious and in search of true fulfilment. They are dismantling our fear that material modesty has to mean degradation and squalor. We can, if we embrace their ideas, live more simply anywhere – including a hut. And in the meantime, we do not need to be so afraid.

ii. How to enjoy a provincial life

There exists in our lives a grand, beguiling, but subtle myth that works its way into the centre of our brains, leading us to judge ourselves calamitous failures and driving us into years of anxious, unrewarding effort and struggle. The myth is constructed around an innocent-sounding, even exciting, idea: the notion that there is a 'centre', a special place on the planet – the right city, or district – and there, and only there, is a real and full life possible. By being exiled from the centre we are condemned to pinched, mediocre existences, cut off from everything important and interesting. We are, we gloomily reflect, mere 'provincials'.

It's a long-standing and surprisingly widespread concept. A thousand years ago, Japanese intellectuals regretted their distance from China – it was only there, they believed, that scholarship, art, poetry and refined manners could flourish. At home, they could only ever be second rate. In the late 19th century, American artists from Massachusetts to Mississippi were tormented by the conviction that their creative life was stunted because they weren't at the centre of cultural life, in Paris. But by the mid-20th century, the people who actually were in Paris felt that only in New York could they live a proper existence and fully participate in the excitements of the modern world. They lamented the tree-lined boulevards and the stately Place des Vosges and dreamed of the East Village and Broadway. In turn, the residents of New York were starting to think that they should really move to California ...

We believe we cannot be content living just anywhere; we gird ourselves to make a bid for life at the 'centre', in one of the world's current hotspots. As a result, we face intense competition and have to work incredibly hard just to survive. Soon we come to think that it's not simply living in the right city that counts; we have to be in the right part, be invited to certain parties, attend particular events and know certain key people.

This harsh contrast between the dull provinces and the glorious centre isn't merely the eccentric preoccupation of a few individuals. There's a surprisingly objective measure to the degree in which a place is considered provincial: property prices. Located in a highly fashionable metropolitan district, a lovely house will command a vast price, while a similarly charming mansion in a pleasant but deeply provincial area will cost only a fraction of the same sum.

We sometimes tell ourselves that the difference is down to other economic factors: in the centre it's possible to earn more, while in the provinces incomes are generally much lower. But the logic is flawed: practically all of the centre-dweller's additional income is spent on covering the expenses of living where they do. Probably they would be better off, financially speaking, if they took a less well-paid post elsewhere. There's no brute material inducement to head to the metropolis; what draws us (and so many others) is a set of 'spiritual' convictions – that is, ideas about the meaning of life.

There are four core beliefs that fuel 'centrism' and drive us to flee the provinces. However, as is often the case, if we go through them one by one and examine them in detail, these ideas turn out to be deeply questionable.

1. People are more interesting
We imagine metropolitan people to be liberated from trivial preoccupations; they don't gossip about

Terraced houses in South Kensington, London. In 2021, houses in this area were on the market for nearly £20 million.

A large, architecturally refined terraced house in a sought-after area of Perth, Scotland. The house was sold in 2021 for under £500,000.

banalities, their minds are occupied by higher thoughts; they're tolerant, intellectually curious and well educated. If we move to the centre, we'll at last meet wonderful people and have fascinating conversations.

Diego Velázquez, *The Waterseller of Seville*, c. 1620

In reality, whether we find someone interesting or not depends more on us than it does on them. Every life, properly engaged with, is endlessly complex, remarkable and informative. In the early 1600s, the

Spanish painter Diego Velázquez painted several portraits of a man who made his very modest living by selling glasses of water to passers-by, from a large earthenware jug he carried with him.

According to the theory of the 'centre', this man is entirely lacking in interest. But Velázquez was entranced. He saw the look on the old man's face as worthy of the same contemplation as the commanding gesture of a victorious general or the gracious curtsy of a lady of the court. In the painting, the man's left hand, touching the water jar, is tender. His right hand, clasping the base of the glass, is deft and delicate. These hands once clutched his mother's hands; they have brushed tears from his cheeks, been joined in prayer, been clenched and shaken in anger.

The painting is a great work of resistance against the centre–provincial divide. Of course interesting people do exist in the centre, but that's because there are interesting people everywhere. What makes the difference isn't where we are, but our mode of engagement.

2. People are more attractive and sophisticated

In our fantasy, metropolitans are more stylish and open-minded. When we get to the centre, we think, we'll finally have the personal life we long for. And yes, perhaps the people in the perfect bar in the centre of town are, superficially, better looking. They may well be dressed in more enticing ways. But these factors – sadly – have little to do with our prospects of intimate happiness.

One reason for this is that what makes someone truly enticing is, in the end, their more elusive and understated qualities: their tone of voice, the way they move their wrist, how they wink at an unexpected moment, their adventurousness, their warmth, when they blush, their curiosity about us. There's no special link between the outward display – at which urbanites may excel – and the subtle elements that can actually bring us contentment.

What's more, no move to the city can save us from the universal sorrows of intimate existence. Whomever we get together with will be (just as we are) extremely difficult to live with in some ways. They'll want to talk when we want to be silent, they'll be too clingy or too distant, they'll be marked by unfortunate episodes in their childhoods. This isn't a problem of where we are; it's a permanent problem of human love that will follow us to the smartest after-parties on the planet and into the most exotic bedrooms.

3. We will be stimulated and inspired

The belief is that those in the centre have bigger ambitions than the provincial hordes; they're engaged in exciting and important quests, and we imagine that this will rub off on us should we join them. We'll visit the same places, breathe the same air that inspired others, and this will fire our own creative capacity.

Simone de Beauvoir and Jean-Paul Sartre, Café de Flore, 1970

However, if we examine more closely the way inspiration works, we will see that it actually follows the reverse. For the entire second half of the 20th century, the most famous café in the world was the Café de Flore in

Paris, where in the 1940s and 1950s, the philosophers Jean-Paul Sartre and Simone de Beauvoir spent many afternoons chatting, writing and drinking coffee; they also loved the boiled egg salad. The temptation is to think that if we were to go there too, our minds would be similarly moved in profound and exciting directions. But if we were to ask Sartre why *he* went there, the answer would be banal: there was nothing special about the place at all, it just happened to be near where he lived. He'd advise us to do the same, or just stick to our room and concentrate on thinking.

It's not that it's impossible to be stimulated in the great urban core – rather it is possible to be inspired anywhere. At root, inspiration is the discovery of the greater meaning of something that seems, initially, unimpressive. One finds potential where others have failed to recognise it. Centrism gets it backwards: it fatally suggests that we should be looking for inspiration in precisely the same places that everyone has already looked.

4. History is being made
The centre is supposedly where all news comes from: it is where important events take place and where new ideas circulate first; the people at the centre are in the know.

This might be the case to some degree, but the reality is that the history that matters to most of us isn't which minister is in favour or what the latest trend in theatre production is or even what the latest evolutions of the fashion industry are. Rather, what we care about are the long-term, overarching and worldwide themes that define the age in which we live – the rise of individualism, the decline of religion, the advancement of capitalism, the retreat of centralised moral authority, the rising prestige of childhood and the falling admiration for science. This kind of history is being made everywhere: the metropolis isn't even the ideal point of observation.

*   *   *

These arguments don't lead to the conclusion that it's impossible to flourish in the metropolis. What they suggest is that the good things associated with the idea of a centre can, in fact, be found pretty much anywhere. What matters isn't so much where you happen to be located, but how you engage with whatever – or whoever – happens to be around. These thoughts liberate us from the imaginary devotion to 'centrism' that does so much to complicate and undermine our brief lives.

iii. Why we need quieter days

For the last two centuries, a cult has been spreading widely and rapidly around the world, seeking to dominate and control every moment of our lives; today it has hundreds of millions of adherents, including almost all the conspicuously successful individuals on the planet. Neither a religious dogma nor a political creed, it is devoted instead to a single, striking ideal: busyness.

This cult of busyness insists that a good life, indeed the only life worthy of a capable and intelligent person, is one of continuous activity and application; we must strive relentlessly to fulfil every ambition, and every hour of the day must be filled with intense activity. A hero of busyness should be up at dawn, following the news on the Shanghai stock exchange; they should jet to Hamburg for a morning meeting (working intensely throughout the journey) and then squeeze in a visit to a seminal exhibition at the

Galerie der Gegenwart at the Hamburger Kunsthalle; in the afternoon they will be back at head office for tough negotiations concerning an urban development project in São Paulo – though they take a quick break for a video chat with their 5-year-old child, who has just had their first violin lesson. In the early evening the hero will drop in on a gala reception at the opera house to have a quick word with the finance minister who is also attending; then there's dinner with a group of major investors, where they can present their strategic overview of next year's expansion in India. Finally, when they get home they will field calls from Boston (medical technology) and Tokyo (intellectual property rights), then sit up late in bed going over papers on tax efficiency and family trusts.

The glamour of this life is constantly reinforced: perhaps there's an admiring article about their business in one of the financial weeklies, or their name is on the wall of the museum as a major benefactor; they see themselves reflected in luxury advertising and the media. Their life is immensely interesting and the whole world, it seems, envies them.

Our own hectic days may not be quite as high-flying, but this is the direction in which they are aiming; if we haven't 'arrived', it's because we haven't tried hard enough – the only thing for it is to push ourselves harder and cram more into each day.

Instead of being blissfully satisfied with our hectic lives, we are liable to feel permanently nervous and strained, though we are careful to conceal this as much as possible from others (and from ourselves). Our irritability is cast as rightful impatience with slackers and mediocrities, and our frustration and disappointment are interpreted as necessary spurs to greater activity. We tell ourselves that our growing gloom and sadness (beneath the zestful demeanour) will disappear when finally we get on top of everything we have to do and attain the level of success that will guarantee our happiness.

More dramatically, we may find we are on the verge (or beyond the verge) of collapse. We may fall ill or suddenly snap and do something disastrous: start screaming during a conference call, become enraged with a lackadaisical junior colleague who then lodges a harassment claim, have an affair or get addicted to drugs 'to unwind'.

The cult of busyness demands that we take on more than we can properly cope with; it ignores or denies our actual fragility until we have a breakdown and want nothing more than to lock ourselves away, smash our phones, lie on the floor and weep.

By contrast, it's moving to think of an attentive mother who settles her child down for an afternoon nap after an exciting morning. The child doesn't know it's worn out, but the mother understands the need for tranquillity and rest. If the child had its way, it would be zooming around the garden, going to another birthday party or watching a frenetic video – before having a tantrum. The maternal function, so to speak, is to calm the child's days, when the child itself is unable or unwilling to recognise its own overwrought state. As adults, we need the maternal part of ourselves to step in and prescribe slower, quieter days – and to rescue us from the oppressive ideal of the busy life, which is slowly destroying us.

The motive for seeking a quieter life is not purely self-preservation, however. Simple days, when nothing much seems to be happening and when we haven't apparently accomplished anything (days the busy person would consider dull and wasted) can be deeply fruitful.

As in the busy life, the perfect quiet day might also start early. From the window we watch the dawn slowly colouring the sky above the houses across the street. We spend part of the morning organising the linen cupboard: folding sheets, stacking blankets, ironing a few napkins and arranging them neatly. Maybe next time we'll go through our wardrobe and weed out the clothes we haven't worn for ages. We're at last bringing order and harmony to our domestic existence.

As we're going about these simple tasks, we can untangle our thoughts and feelings. When we're preoccupied, we don't properly notice the details of our emotional state or what's going on at the back of our minds. Now we can start to pay closer attention: why did we fall out with that friend last year? Was it, perhaps, that we never particularly liked each other anyway? What did we really feel in their company? Who, ideally, would we like to be friends with? And what is it about them that appeals to us?

In the afternoon, we might take a long walk, alone. We pass an old brick wall that we'd hardly noticed before. It's been weathered by the sun and the rain and delicately spotted with yellow lichen: how long has it been there, and what happened to the people who built it? It was probably rather stark and raw originally; time has been kind to it.

Perhaps we pause to look carefully at a tree; the branches look bare, but close up we can see the first, tiny tips of green starting to emerge from some of the brown buds. In the past we only ever noted the big changes; now we're registering the beautiful, minute steps, accomplished day by day, that take us from one season to another.

In our slow days we have the time, and the patience, to notice what at first seem like small sources of pleasure. As we appreciate them, we are able to realise how important and moving they really are – and how much we missed out on when, in our busier time, we tried to do everything.

After a light supper, we lie soaking in a hot, deep bath. As our body relaxes and our mind is soothed, we meditate on what we really want to do with our lives. In place of the conventional aspirations that used to drive us, we might become sensitive to our own authentic ambitions. It could be nice to take up drawing; how might our relationship with our mother be improved; what kind of work gives us most satisfaction; what kind of fruitful relationships might be possible? We can dig around in the neglected territory of our needs and longings and begin to think through how they could realistically evolve.

At the end of our quiet day, we turn in early, so we'll be fresh in the morning. In the minutes before we sleep, we go over the memories of a trip from years ago: recapturing the charming manners of a particular waiter or the pleasure of opening the shutters in the morning and looking down a narrow street towards the sea; we're planning to stay quietly put for a while and we don't need to go anywhere – our lives are rich and large already.

iv. How to go to bed earlier

There's a pattern that goes like this: it's late, given when we've got to wake up in the morning, but instead of going to bed, we stay up. The next day, of course, we feel sluggish and weary and we promise ourselves an early night. Then it happens again: it's already midnight and we have work the next day, but we don't turn in. It's not that we're full of energy – we actually feel desperately tired – but we resist going to bed. The following day it's the same: we're worn out, yet we don't go to bed until far later than we should. And it keeps on going.

At times during this cycle we feel deeply frustrated. We call ourselves idiots and worse. Obviously, we need to get to bed early, yet we are too stupid, stubborn and self-sabotaging to do so. To our profound exhaustion we add the burden of self-disgust – but our anger at our own behaviour doesn't lead us to change our habits. If our partner complains about our late hours, we dismiss it as nagging – and it's all the more irritating because we know they are right.

It's one of the strangest features of being human: we have a completely clear sense that how we're behaving is bad and counterproductive, but it doesn't get us to stop. Harsh criticism is the utterly entrenched human tactic for getting people to change, just as self-condemnation is our instinctive strategy for self-improvement – yet it doesn't actually work. It induces panic, shame and despair but doesn't bring about the desired alteration.

A gentler – and more productive – approach begins with curiosity: it takes the difficult matter of behaviour seriously and asks what it wants and what it is seeking. It seems foreign, and almost irresponsible, to ask the key question: *what's nice about staying up late?* Why, really, are we doing it? We shy away from this question because it seems counterproductive to suggest that there could be anything interesting or good about an action that's clearly messing up our lives. So, what might we be *trying to achieve* by staying up late?

For many years throughout our childhood, night-time seemed immensely exciting. It was a secret, mysterious zone, when from our dark room we might hear grown-ups laughing around the dinner table, talking of things we weren't supposed to know about. If we were ever allowed to be up late it would usually be for a very special occasion: a New Year's Eve party at Granny's house, when bearded great-uncles would slip us chocolates and we'd crowd into a cousin's bedroom to watch a film, or a thrilling late-night flight at the start of an overseas holiday, when the world seemed enormous and filled with adventure.

Later, in adolescence and as students, the night became glamorous; it was when poets found their inspiration, when parties became wild, when our friends were the most enthusiastic in their plans to reform the world – and when we finally kissed our first love.

Even though such positive associations may not be at the front of our minds, we continue to harbour a buried, but significant, sense that to go to bed early is to miss out on the joys of existence. Our late-night activities might be utterly prosaic, but just by being awake into the early hours we feel that we're participating in an ideal of what adult life is supposed to be like. And so, night after night, the bed is there, quietly waiting for us to draw back the sheet, turn out the light, lie down and close our eyes, but it's past midnight and we're still up.

At these times, we must look on ourselves with tenderness. We're not idiots because we stay up into the night; we're just in search of something important. The problem isn't what we're looking for but the fact that we can't find it this way. The thrills that have implanted themselves in our memories were only linked to being up late by accident. The conviviality, the sense of discovery and adventure, the feeling of exploring big ideas and the experience of emotional intimacy have no intrinsic connection to the hours of darkness. The deeper engagement with a friend or a lover, the working through of a complex idea, the determination to investigate a neglected area of our potential: these aren't late-night speculations; they are the tasks of our daytime selves – requiring for their proper accomplishment our poised and well-rested minds.

We will at last be able to turn in early – and get the sleep we need – not when our irritation with ourselves reaches an unbearable peak and we finally submit to the banality of an early bedtime, but when we seek our pleasures where they can more realistically be found: in the bright, energetic hours of the new day.

v. How to be a modern monk

Monasticism – with its signature haircuts, long robes, cloisters, ritual fasting and heavy prayer schedules – has been in existence around the world for many centuries. It's unlikely, however, to cross our minds today as a remotely plausible career path: it's too bound up with hard-to-believe doctrines about the need for sexual abstinence, the survival of the soul after death and the will of God.

Yet in a limited, though significant and very unexpected, way we perhaps do wish to become more like monks. That's because at its core (if we strip away the elaborate theology) monasticism points to a moving ideal: the possibility of uniting simplicity with dignity. It fuses minimalistic external presentation with beauty and spiritual elevation.

Cloister, Franciscan Church and Monastery, Dubrovnik, Croatia

In a good monastic life, the food might be plain, but it is nourishing and carefully prepared; a monk's room may be almost bare, but the furnishings are well made; the common areas are restrained but elegant; the monks have little or no money, but their days are tranquil, focused and well organised. Rather than feeling humiliated by their modest possessions, small and unadorned rooms and lack of personal wealth, monks have a deep conviction in the legitimacy and worth of their existence.

The union of simplicity with dignity is a beguiling idea, but in the modern world this combination has come to look impossible. In our commercial and highly competitive societies, a very limited material life suggests failure and squalor: unhealthy, industrialised fast food, poor-quality clothing, shoddy furniture, ugly, mass-produced housing, social chaos and marginalisation.

There is a neglected strand of modernist thought, however, that strives to make simple dignity more readily available – insisting that a materially modest life is capable of being rendered noble and fulfilling. This ambition was explicitly articulated by the Swiss-French architect Le Corbusier, who, in his 1923 book, *Towards a New Architecture*, declared: 'What [modern man] wants is a monk's cell, well-lit and heated, with a corner from which he can look at the stars.'

For Le Corbusier, this wasn't just a poetic fantasy; he put this idea into practice repeatedly, in the furniture and housing he designed across his career. His most advanced attempt to create a modern, secular 'monastery' came with the construction of a large apartment block, the Cité Radieuse, in Marseilles, France, in the 1950s.

Le Corbusier, apartment in the Cité Radieuse, Marseilles, 1952

Le Corbusier, living room in the Cité Radieuse, Marseilles, 1952.
Every element of the design creates an atmosphere of dignified calm.

In Le Corbusier's block, a standard apartment is made up of just a single main room, with the bed located on a suspended mezzanine above (family apartments are slightly larger). However, the space is so well thought through that it does not feel mean or cramped. The styling is emphatically clean: straight lines, with no cornices or skirting boards. Though narrow, the sitting area is lofty; a large, high window fills one end and an external overhang keeps out the glare, so that the whole place is filled with a bright, but even, daylight.

Le Corbusier envisaged an uncluttered interior in keeping with the architecture. Just a few serviceable but solidly made pieces, many of which he designed: a low daybed, a small table, a couple of chairs and perhaps a neutral-coloured woven mat on the floor. If you had the *right* things, he argued, you wouldn't need many things.

Le Corbusier was also inspired by another feature of monasticism: the emphasis on communal life. On the wide, flat roof of his apartment block, he installed a running track, an amphitheatre for meetings and plays, a crèche, a small swimming pool and a large sunbathing terrace, as well as dining areas where residents could eat together.

Le Corbusier, The Cité Radieuse crèche, located in a
pavilion on the roof of the building

Le Corbusier envisaged his apartment as a 'machine
for living', a statement that invites us to translate
the principles of clean, simple architecture into the
ordinary details of everyday life.

What do they have on the walls?

In a monastery, a monk would have a religious icon or
perhaps a crucifix on the wall – not just for decoration,
but to symbolise their devotion to God and give them a
visual reminder of why they live in this way.

An ideal option for a modern, secular equivalent
might be a print of one of Pablo Picasso's drawings

of birds, which he produced around the same time as Le Corbusier was working. He drew these in his studio, half an hour's drive away from Marseilles in the commune of Vauvenargues, near Aix-en-Provence.

Pablo Picasso, *Dove*, 1961

At this late stage in his career (he was nearing eighty), Picasso was making a large number of simple line drawings, in which he omitted almost all naturalistic features. We do not see the precise number and shape of the tail feathers, the exact way the wings connect to the body or the variations in colouring across the back and chest. Instead, with just a few quick strokes, he sought to create a sense of lightness, movement and freedom. The picture shares a common goal with

Le Corbusier's building: it was interested in how much one can leave out, while getting quickly and directly to the most important and essential components.

What's in the kitchen?

In the original Le Corbusier apartment, there was a compact cooking range designed by his collaborator Charlotte Perriand. But what kinds of meals would the modern monk eat, in keeping with the restrained and refined aesthetic of the flat? If we looked in the fridge and the cupboards, what would we find?

Rather than sacks of potatoes, packets of pasta and slabs of oven-ready pizza, perhaps we would find a selection of nuts, some cheese, a bowl of fruit and a few slices of ham: food for grazing on, that require almost no preparation and leave very little washing up to be done. Choosing these simple foods liberates our lives, and our storage space, from pots and pans, blenders and pressure cookers. They appeal to the quick, light pleasures of the palate rather than the heavy fullness of the stomach – they are the culinary equivalent of a modernist steel and leather sofa.

What's in the wardrobe?

Typical monastic clothing looks quite strange to us

now, but that's an effect of unchanging tradition. When the long, dark robes were first selected – by St Benedict, around the year CE 500 – they were merely sober, plain – but good-quality – versions of what people would normally wear. The aim wasn't to make the monk look conspicuous or odd, but to free them from having to think or worry about what to wear.

So, what might we find if we opened the wardrobe of a Le Corbusier apartment, built into the wall next to the bed on the mezzanine level? We would likely find just a few well-chosen pieces (maybe two or three of each type) in a standard colour (perhaps dark blue). This has nothing to do with self-deprivation – the clothes may well be beautifully designed and perfectly tailored – but the result is that the resident rarely has to go shopping, and need never tax their minds with the question of what to put on.

What's on the bookshelves?
In a traditional cell, a monk would only have had a handful of books. Their view on reading is somewhat at odds with our current vision of culture. Today, the cultured person is imagined as possessing a substantial personal library – whatever book is mentioned in conversation, they should be able to find a copy

somewhere on their many shelves. The monastic ideal, by contrast, prefers an intimate relationship with a very limited number of 'sacred' works, which eventually the monk will know almost by heart. Likewise, the modern monk has only a few books in their apartment. They prioritise depth over extensive, random browsing. As with the stomach, it's not the quantity of matter that passes through our brains that feeds or cultivates us; it's how we digest it.

*   *   *

The appeal of this monkish simplicity is that it has a positive, rather than a negative, motive. Rather than miserably forgoing the comforts of life, as we might expect, the aim is deliberately to seek out what we are really interested in, helped by or excited by – and to pare down our life so as to let what really counts finally emerge.

vi. Good materialism

One of our strongest instincts when considering how to achieve a simpler life is to move away from what is termed 'materialism'. It's hardly a surprise that we latch onto this analysis of our troubles: the case against materialism has been building for a long time. If we believe what we are told, then materialism is the enemy of spiritual life – it corrupts our instincts, leads us to prioritise property over people, makes us callous, greedy and self-centred, destroys communities, breeds inequality and injustice, starts wars, alienates us from nature and ultimately destroys the planet. The verdict looks plain: we have individually and collectively lost our way because we love our possessions too much. That's why the world is awful.

With all this in mind, it might seem absurd – and even morally deranged – to stick up for materialism and suggest that a deep attachment to objects has an important, central role to play in a well-lived, flourishing life; that materialism can be not merely a stubborn flaw in our characters that we have to tame and overcome, but something that can be positively admirable and constructive.

To begin to explore how this is possible, we should consider a subject on which even a devoted antimaterialist could understand a devotion to objects: religion. For example, take this slightly larger than life-sized bronze head, made around 600 years ago in what is now Nigeria.

Unknown Yoruba artist, *The Ife Head*, c. 14th–15th century

It's a sacred object that conveys an ideal of dignity and authority. If we were to imagine the head speaking, it might say something like this:

I don't get distracted easily – I concentrate on what I know is important, even though this could strike others as verging on ruthlessness, but it's what you've got to do to get things done. I'm not timid, but I'm not arrogant; rather, I confidently assert what I think because I've thought it through. I've learnt a lot from experience and from the many challenges I've had to face: I'm going to state plainly and clearly what I think. I want to look you in the eye and can bear you being honest with me.

For a sensitive and intelligent beholder, this is a powerful, urgent message: we need the qualities of focus and calm confidence that are embodied in this object of supreme beauty in our own lives.

All religions are obsessed by a standard weakness of the human mind: we forget in practice the important things that, in theory, we know already. The person paying homage to the bronze head already 'knows' that they dither, procrastinate and hold back from self-assertion – but their leaky brain requires constant reinforcement. Material objects – silent though they are

– can be eloquent sources of important psychological messages; they can prompt, encourage, upbraid and generally remind us of our better selves – and by doing so they make a powerful, positive contribution to our lives.

It's not only sacred objects that can do this. We have only a feeble, intermittent hold on our better insights and we require physical things to function as holders and transmitters of the more mature, wiser and, at points, nicer versions of who we can be. We can see this abstract idea played out across the details of our own material lives.

Honouring the form of everyday items might seem utterly at odds with the pursuit of a simpler, more elevated existence. But imagine what these particular examples might have to say to us:

1. A dinner plate

Wedgwood plate with moulded lobed decoration on the rim, c. 1780–1795

For the most part I'm quite plain – but that's not my whole story; around my edges I'm distinctly playful. We might discuss serious issues, but you'll catch a hint of a warm smile; if someone is being boring, I won't rudely interrupt them, but I'll give you a sly wink to show I understand. I'm sober and sweet – and invite you to be so as well.

2. A daybed

Mies van der Rohe, Barcelona daybed, 1930

I'm not lazy, though I do value rest and repose. I know that serious thinking is hard – we forget how taxing it is on the body. Sometimes what's needed is to have a lie-down – that's when the resistance to big ideas starts to fall away. I'm not merely an addition to the world of interior decoration; I'm a modern aid to self-exploration and imagination.

3. A dress

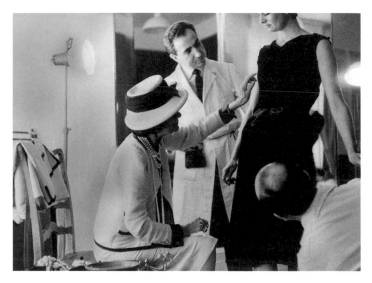

Coco Chanel adjusting a detail on one of her classic black dresses, 1962

I'm interested in equality – I like the idea that elegance should be more easily attainable and therefore widespread; I don't show off, but I am quietly confident.

4. A bowl

Porcelain bowl with *kintsugi* repair

I've been broken, but it wasn't the end of the world; I was fixed and the evidence of the repair adds to my beauty. Failing, getting it wrong, messing up, having to climb down, being the one who has to say sorry – that's not humiliation; it's part of what makes people attractive. The name of my repair, kintsugi, means 'golden joinery'.

5. A jacket

A classic men's suit jacket

I know plenty of people don't, but I enjoy a touch of formality. It's not because I'm cold or stuffy; rather, it's a kind of politeness. Not everyone has time for, or is interested in, their raw selves.

6. A door handle

Door handle in Haus Wittgenstein, Vienna, completed in 1928

I might not look like anything special, but a lot of thought and careful work went into making me (I was designed by a philosopher, Ludwig Wittgenstein – see page 87). I consider the needs of others without losing my integrity; you'll find I'm perfectly adjusted to your grip and I close with a satisfying, solid 'click'.

7. A wardrobe

A built-in sectional wardrobe

I enjoy being organised. It's not a boring duty; it's a source of beauty and the basis of all achievement.

8. A desk lamp

Anglepoise lamp, c. 1960

I don't try to light up the whole room; I'd rather focus on something constructive and specific. Getting the angle and intensity right is important to me.

*   *   *

The possession – and love – of a few objects like these is in a sense 'materialistic': we're attracted to them and are proud to own them – indeed, we love them even though they are simply brute 'stuff'. But they each provide something we deeply need in order to flourish properly, so our attachment to them moves far beyond the greedy or the ostentatious. It's this crucial dimension of our relationship with possessions that's neglected by the understandable, but over-hasty, dismissal of all attachment to purchases as 'materialistic'.

Ironically, it turns out that 'bad' materialism isn't really an excessive fondness for objects and possessions; rather, it stems from a failure to appreciate objects properly. Truly 'good' materialism leads us to want fewer things and to choose them with care, while bad materialism results in us filling our homes with needless stuff that we have no room for in our hearts. We clutter up our wardrobes, homes and lives because the messages our possessions are sending us aren't being listened to.

If we possess – and pay attention to – the few things we really love, we'll not need very many of them. Imagine it like having a great conversation with one precious person, which is far more rewarding than trying to chat with twenty other people who are all saying different things at the same time. The material objects that really speak to us need time and space to get their messages across to us. We become more sparing and selective in adding possessions when we are properly attuned to the contributions that material things can make to our lives. The solution to the ills of materialism – and the path to a less muddled and chaotic home – isn't renunciation; it's a deeper and more selective kind of love.

IV.

Work and Simplicity

i. Thinking rather than doing

Paradoxically, the human brain – which as the organ for thought could be assumed to love this activity above any other – seems to operate with a firm bias in favour of action over reflection.

This may be explained by evolution. We started out as – and hence largely remain – creatures that needed to get things done rather than ponder why we were doing them. We had to follow the herd, sow the crops and flee from predators – and those individuals who stopped to contemplate the meaning of life were generally left with slim chances of survival. Our early ancestors were not, on the whole, philosophers.

Like all powerful prejudices, we don't openly announce our hostility to thinking either to ourselves or others. But in our conduct, and in society at large, the priority is clear: activity counts for infinitely more than intellectual enquiry. This bias is particularly demonstrated in the way our working lives have come to be organised; here there is a blatant emphasis on visible effort over background reflection. We are measured by the number of hours we have put in, the length of the meetings we have attended, the complexity of the forms we have processed and the accumulation of countries we have visited. Our shared valorisation of tangible, action-focused work gets a sly boost from the often unimpressive performance of professed 'thinkers': the intellectual 'egghead' is readily cast as aloof, maddeningly abstract and hopelessly impractical. We might not want to admit out loud that thinking is useless, but, sadly and privately, it strikes us as being close to exactly that.

This is something of a tragedy, because most of what goes wrong in our lives is not due to a failure of raw effort or busyness. We come to grief not because we haven't rushed around enough or put in a sufficient number of hours at the coalface, but because there has, somewhere along the way, been a shortfall in thinking. We do not allow ourselves the requisite number of hours in which we might – to a critical outside eye – look as if we were doing 'nothing': gazing out of the window, following a trail of clouds across the evening sky, lying in a bath, walking around a park or writing down a few notes in a journal. It is precisely during these apparently empty hours of reflection that life's real work unfolds – hours in which our worst mistakes can be caught, and our best opportunities identified.

Thinking is, unfortunately, extremely painful – far more so even than getting up early to catch a train or scheduling yet more meetings into an already packed day. It requires immense bravery to ask ourselves difficult questions about our intentions and goals, including those concerning our work life; to wonder, for example, what we are truly trying to do with our colleagues, or whom a given product or service might actually be of use to.

Most businesses and work schemes fail not because people have been physically lazy, but because they have omitted to pass their plans through the robust sieve of their own intelligence. Eventually, all ideas will be judged by reality; what thinking allows us to do is anticipate problems before they have grown too large and too costly. By sitting in bed for an extra hour with a pen and paper, we can stress-test our plans long before they make fateful contact with an impatient and highly competitive world.

It might sound easy enough to do this, but it is in truth an arduous process to deliberately subject our most cherished thoughts and exciting projects to relentless, hostile crossfire. Good thinking requires us to put ourselves on both sides of an argument, considering the *contra* case as imaginatively and creatively as we do the *pro*. We must move from the charming initial suggestion to a cynical objection, then to the formation of a new stance that has been intelligently revised by opposition – and on and on through continuing rounds of refinement until, through a dialectical sequence of mental battles, we start to home in on a mature, workable version of our initial hunch.

If we are thinking constructively, then along the way we'll have to do something else that feels uncomfortable: put ourselves in the shoes of others. We tend not to notice the unfortunate degree to which we instinctively suppose that others must – really – be like us, and will therefore share our enthusiasms and loves. Yet many disasters in the world of work might be avoided if people were to reflect, honestly and profoundly, on how an audience other than themselves might feel about a service or product.

In a more thinking-supportive culture, it would be normal to be suspicious of very busy people – and to be admiring of those who might spend days, weeks or even years apparently not doing much other than daydreaming, only eventually to deliver something of outstanding value and importance. We could give greater legitimacy to outward simplicity and non-activity in the name of critical analysis. Along the way, we might grow more curious about the things that help us to think well – that coax and encourage the mind to be hard on its favourite ideas and to place itself in the position of people who are not like us. Long baths in the afternoon might be advisable, as might midmorning naps. Cooking soup or sitting on a park bench might become important, highly respected parts of 'working' life – for these are periods when, as the body is soothed or distracted, the deeper parts of our intelligence can come to the fore. Just as when traffic stops, we can hear the sounds of birds or the rustling of leaves in the breeze, so when we stop having to attend to immediate inner alarms, the quieter, more ambitious and braver suggestions of our minds can be attended to.

A thinking culture is not one without achievement; it is one that properly understands the role played by good *thinking* in the delivery of good *doing*. Working life might look much less productive from the outside, but in reality we would be locating true hard work where it actually has to unfold: inside our own minds.

ii. Voluntary poverty

A distinctive feature of modern life is the extent to which we devote it to making – or aspiring to make – money. We worry about money as we approach the end of our education, we worry about it throughout our working years and we worry about it in retirement. A large part of our brief mental life is made up of anxious thoughts about our financial position.

However, it's important to understand that our worry about money is – in most countries at this point in history – typically disconnected from any issues of survival. We could keep going on much less than we have – as almost everyone who ever lived has done. What drives us to accumulate is a psychological necessity, not a material one. We are under the sway of a powerful cultural force: our ability to think well of ourselves has become equated with an ability to generate an impressive income. Earning healthy sums isn't so much practically important as emotionally significant; it's grown to be our chief marker of decency. We operate with the background conviction that a failure to make money could only arise from some form of moral and metaphysical inadequacy: poverty must be a sign that someone is too unreliable, self-indulgent, timid, irresponsible or stupid to thrive in the marketplace.

And yet, history reveals plenty of highly instructive examples of people who made deliberate, unapologetic decisions to embrace a modest income in the name of other goals; people who managed to think well of themselves despite being poorer than they might have been.

These people are followers of a concept known as 'voluntary poverty'. If the term sounds paradoxical, or even perverse, it is because our own era has difficulty imagining that anyone could sanely enter into a *voluntary* relationship with something as appalling as having little money. We can only picture ourselves as having to *bravely put up* with poverty, never as choosing it.

The outstanding representative of voluntary poverty in the Classical period was the Roman statesman Lucius

Quinctius Cincinnatus (c. 519–c. 430 BCE), in honour of whom the US city of Cincinnati is named. Cincinnatus came from a prestigious, but impoverished, family; he'd had a very successful public career, but, being honourable and very honest, had never made any money out of his service. Tiring of the shabby deals and devious self-seeking of his colleagues, he retired early to a small farm, where he worked his own land and eked out a modest living.

Alexandre Cabanel, *Cincinnatus Receiving the Ambassadors of Rome*, 1843. The noble Cincinnatus – bare-chested – weighs up whether to remain a simple farmer or head the Roman state.

At this point, Rome was still a republic – but a far from mighty one. In 458 BCE, as had often happened before, one of the neighbouring tribes launched a major invasion that threatened to annihilate the state. In desperation, a government envoy was dispatched to Cincinnatus, begging him to return to Rome, where he could adopt unlimited powers and see off the threat. Cincinnatus was ploughing his field bare-chested when the envoy arrived. He considered the offer for a few minutes, weighing up his longing for a quiet, agricultural life against the urgent needs of his nation, and then asked his wife, Racilia, to fetch his toga from their simple cottage. He accepted the role of temporary dictator and rapidly succeeded in repelling the attack on Rome. Given his triumph, everything was now open to him: Cincinnatus could have held onto his position as dictator and accumulated boundless wealth. But this was not his way. He loved his family and his life as a farmer far too much. So, he resigned and returned home to his plough and his few acres. He chose voluntary poverty over luxury and grandeur.

What motivated Cincinnatus was an intelligent and discerning sense of what truly brought him contentment. Marble palaces and gold might have carried prestige, but when Cincinnatus examined his subjective sources of pleasure, he realised that what actually satisfied him was getting up early in the morning to water his oxen, watching his fields slowly ripen and chatting with his wife and children after a physically exhausting but rewarding day under the sun. Cincinnatus' enduring legacy was to be a man of opportunity who took the trouble to realise that there were things he loved more than money.

As a modern example, the Canadian artist Agnes Martin (1912–2004) also discovered that she had concerns beyond the pursuit of wealth. After college, rather than seeking properly paid employment, Martin began an itinerant life, first in the USA, then Canada and the deserts of New Mexico. There she built herself – largely by her own hands – a tiny, mud-brick house. She lived in an austere fashion, wearing only the most functional clothes, subsisting on a bare diet of cheese and fruit, and paying no attention at all to money – devoting herself instead to producing some of the simplest and most beautiful works of art ever made. Ironically, by the end of her life, Martin had accumulated enormous sums through her paintings, each of which sold for many millions of dollars. But she couldn't care less; a treat for her was to head to a local diner to have an omelette with a friend.

Agnes Martin, *Affection*, 2001

It wasn't so much that Martin hated money, but that she had discovered something far more precious to her than material accumulation. She treasured the gentle tranquillity of mind that she experienced when creating her artworks – canvases made up of repeated rhythmic patterns and lines against coloured backgrounds, delicate pencil marks interspersed with bands of muted pinks or blues.

Our preoccupation with money feels highly respectable, but its true cause is poignant and unexpected: we keep wanting more money because we haven't yet identified a passion that matters enough to us that it replaces money-making in our minds. Most of us haven't found what farming was to Cincinnatus or painting was to Martin; we haven't yet discovered the real reasons why we are alive.

It's not that we don't each have such reasons – they are inside us and always have been. We carry within us a range of authentic allegiances for which we would be willing, in theory, to give up much of our financial appetite. Passions are not only for a few, highly unusual individuals; we all have them and used to engage with them regularly when we were small children who knew how to play. It is simply that the prevailing ideology of modernity doesn't invite us to work out what our passions might be. Nothing in our education system allows us to imagine that the root of genuine contentment and freedom may lie in discovering the few things that matter more to us than money.

It's understandable to be nervous about untethering ourselves, even to a limited extent, from the conventional views that link money and our worth as individuals. It is painfully normal to be terrified of how others will react should we fail to produce a standard, respectable answer to the question 'What do you do?' We have learnt to doubt our right to lead the kinds of lives we long for and deserve.

Our fear of that difficult question suggests the path we can take to free ourselves. The clearer we can be in our own minds as to our true passions, the more we can start to see money (and the socially sanctioned praise it brings with it) from a realistic perspective. Money is a mechanism or a means that, at best, enables us to do the things we love, nothing more or less. It is not, or should not, be a route to liking ourselves, or an end in itself.

We will be able to choose poverty voluntarily – to freely forgo luxuries, comforts and the prestige of being prosperous – once we focus our lives on what deeply matters to us. We will fall out of love with money the more we learn to fall in love with something else: farming, music, service, writing, God, quiet evenings at home or the painting of slow, delicate lines across pale pink canvases.

iii. The terror of simplicity

One of the reasons we fear a simple, financially modest life is that we rarely take the trouble calmly to examine what it might really be like, and so we are inclined to fear it far more than we should.

The Roman philosopher, banker and tutor Seneca (c. 4 BCE–65 CE) did just the opposite. By midlife he was not only prosperous but distinctly wealthy, having risen to a senior position in the heart of the imperial government. However, while rich, Seneca was keen never to let the thought of poverty frighten him. So, in his large town house, next to his magnificent bedroom, Seneca built a small chamber not unlike a prison cell. Once a week or so he would sleep there, on a bare bunk, eating only old bread and olives and drinking water. This activity was part of what he called a 'premeditation' – a rehearsal of what it would be like actually to face his fears. 'We suffer more often in imagination than in reality,' he wrote. Seneca understood that by making ourselves think carefully and in detail about what we dread, we can reduce our fears to their correct and manageable proportions.

Inspired by this example, we might undertake a 'premeditation' ourselves, taking into account our own anxieties around simplicity.

If we were to 'come down in the world', it's likely true that certain acquaintances would drop us; they'd make it clear that we were no longer good enough for them. But in doing so, they would prove that, in fact, they had never been decent enough for us. Other friends, conversely, wouldn't be so changed in their views of us, for our success wasn't what drew them to us in the first place: they like us for our sense of humour, our views on life, our curiosity or our warm sympathy for *their* troubles – all of which would still be intact.

It might equally be true that, if things were to go badly, we wouldn't be able to afford to live anywhere distinguished. Thankfully, however, we can be sure that, in reality, wherever we ended up, we would have some interesting and kindly neighbours. The reasons for this are fundamental: goodwill, decency and sympathy are not confined to a particular socio-economic bracket.

As for our pleasures, while we might no longer be able to take in the first night at the opera, there would be so much else left. We might have to read a tattered paperback, but we can still spend time with Tolstoy or Epicurus. Perhaps we would need to live for a week on what we used to pay for one lunch – but there would still be nature, kindness and love.

There is a strain of social conscience that makes us feel it should be morally wrong to say that life on a modest income could be acceptable. To say this might sound as if we were thereby condoning extreme deprivation. But in truth, we are able get by in a much simpler way than at first seems possible.

Society has been very good at explaining to us the pleasures and attractions of success. In film – the most potent medium of the last hundred years – the great narratives are upward trajectories, rags-to-riches stories that trace a character's path from a lowly position to one of power and influence. The art we really need is that which follows the opposite arc – celebrating people who downshifted, adjusted, but still endured and prospered internally.

Involuntary simplification frightens us more than it should because we've constructed for ourselves inaccurate ideas of what a basic life would really entail. By exploring realistic versions, we can increase our courage and reduce our wilder panics. We can tap into the basic truth that throughout history almost everyone lived a more materially modest life than we currently do. Their lives weren't worthless or pointless, and nor will ours be – even if what we fear does ever come to pass.

Culture and Simplicity

i. How to be less pretentious

There are stock images of what a 'pretentious' person might be like: someone who recites lines of Latin poetry, makes references to German philosophy, wears a cravat and perhaps carries a gold-tipped cane on their perambulations. Most of us are happy to conclude that we do not in any way belong to this questionable and dated category. We pride ourselves on our modernity and straightforwardness.

Yet, despite our casual demeanour and lack of intimacy with Virgil or Heidegger, we may remain pretentious in the true and essential sense of the term; that is, we *pretend – far more regularly than we should – to be more sophisticated, stylish and in the know than we actually are*. We're not attempting to fool others in a directly egregious way – we're not inventing qualifications or distorting our CV – but what we are often doing, in a multitude of minor instances, is ceasing to listen closely to our own authentic responses. Whether it's our opinion on books, holiday destinations, acquaintances, leisure pursuits or political views, we find ourselves deferring to, and parroting, the attitudes of established and prestigious others.

'Pretentiously' we declare a dance track that left us cold to be just what we like; we dress in sportswear that feels tight and itchy to us but is held to be fashionable by a stylish elite; we cook friends elaborate meals when we would much prefer a boiled egg; we declare a baffling piece of video art 'extremely thought-provoking'; we feign agreement with progressive political ideas that terrify us with their intolerance and self-righteousness; if we write – a report, thesis or even a piece of creative writing – our style becomes stilted, as it never would in a private message to a friend.

It is noteworthy that our pretension tends to go in one direction only: away from simplicity and towards complexity. Our culture almost always prompts us to ditch our simpler, plainer, more homely instincts (for songs with a rhythm to them, for books you can understand, for food that is tasty and quick to prepare, for politics imbued with common sense) and to force ourselves into alignment with more abstruse and elusive attitudes.

Rather than blame ourselves for being spineless, we might ask ourselves why we tend to back away from our own preferences. As is often the case, the reason is fear. We lie because we worry about how we would be judged if what we actually liked was revealed. Behind this fear usually lies a certain sort of childhood: the archetypal upbringing of the pretentious adult. Here, at formative moments, our caregivers and educators gave us the impression that our own thoughts and feelings were wholly inadequate and unreliable guides to life: we didn't know enough, we were in no position to decide, we were too young. The message could be delivered harshly or gently, but it was still the same: we should defer to the 'proper' views of others. We were taught to be ashamed of our spontaneous responses.

We were made to understand that the museum *was* actually very interesting, learning geography *was* important, lining up stones in the garden *was* silly, crying over Teddy's torn arm *was* babyish, putting jam on cheese crackers *was* wrong and talking at length to our imaginary friend about the future *was* – definitely – crazy.

From such commentary, we slowly picked up a sense that we were not to trust ourselves as arbiters of taste. We acquired the building blocks for our future intellectual deference. These messages are why – twenty years later – we might pretend to love Joey Bada$$, the architecture of Rem Koolhaas or the novels of W.G. Sebald.

By contrast, it's possible to imagine a set of ideal early experiences that would insulate someone from the need to pretend and that would encourage honesty and directness. From our first years, our responses would be treated with respect. Our pleasures and dislikes would be discussed with interest; we'd be invited to describe what we felt and to be curious about why we liked or rejected something. We'd be warmly encouraged to develop and expand our particular enthusiasms, even if they were rather odd. We'd be given a chance to design our own meals or decorate a room the way we liked. We'd be allowed to question received opinions without being humiliated; whether others agreed wouldn't be held up as the decisive factor. Sometimes we would be in the majority, sometimes in the minority; occasionally we would find ourselves in a constituency of one. Our likings might seem too highbrow to some and too lowbrow – or even wildly eccentric – to others, but we'd be shown that that didn't matter at all. We'd hear from people we respect that no one really knows what's right and wrong and that everyone is a bit silly at heart. We would be able to deduce that the point of life isn't to have the 'right' reactions, just our own, very honest, ones.

Even without the luxury of such a childhood, our tendency to pretension can be quietened once we recognise – without shame – that we are liable to feel pressured into distorting our authentic enjoyments because of an early vulnerability. We can start to notice the times when we abandon our true enthusiasms – and become aware of our own histories, and the details of them that influenced our need to have the 'right' preferences. Once we do this, we'll be in a position to discover who we really are in the world of culture; and, to our surprise and delight, it might be someone a lot simpler and more easily satisfied than we had ever imagined.

ii. How to read fewer books

The modern world firmly equates the intelligent person with the well-read person. Reading books – a lot of books – is understood as the hallmark of brilliance and the supreme gateway to knowledge and prestige. It's hard to imagine anyone arriving at an insight of value without having worked through an enormous number of titles over the years. There is apparently no limit to how much we should read. Ideally, we would read all the time, getting cleverer with every moment – after which the number of books we managed to read by the day we die would tell us pretty much all we needed to know about the complexity and maturity of our minds.

This maximalist philosophy of reading enjoys great cultural prestige. It is backed up by publishing and journalistic industries that constantly parade new titles before us – implying that we will be swiftly left behind and condemned to a narrow and provincial mindset if we don't rush to read this year's major prize-winning books and other well-reviewed titles. As a result, our shelves are overburdened and our guilt for being behind is ever more intense.

Amidst this pressure, we should pause to reflect on a fascinating aspect of the premodern world: people were not under pressure to read very much at all. Reading was held to be extremely important, but the *number* of new books one read was inconsequential. We might imagine this to be a principally economic issue, but that is not the case. Books were very expensive, of course, but what really mattered at the time was to read a few books very well – not squander one's attention promiscuously on a great number of volumes.

The thinkers of the premodern world cared so little about the quantity of books one read because they were obsessed by a question that modernity likes to dodge: *what is the point of reading?* And they had answers. To take a supreme example, Christians and Muslims located the value of reading in a very specific and narrow goal: the attainment of holiness. To read was to try to approximate the mind of God. In each case this meant that one book – and one book only, the Bible or the Koran – was held up as vastly and incomparably more important than any other. To read this book, repeatedly and with great attention, was thought more crucial than to rush through a whole library every week; in fact, reading widely would have been regarded with suspicion, because most other books would – to some extent – have been thought misleading and distracting.

Similarly, in the ancient Greek world, readers were encouraged to focus on gaining a close knowledge of just two books: Homer's *Odyssey* and *Iliad*. These books were deemed the perfect repository of the Greek code of honour and the best guides to action in military and civilian affairs. Much later, in 18th-century England, the ideal of reading came to be focused on Virgil's *Aeneid*. Knowing this epic poem by heart was all a gentleman needed to do to pass as cultivated. To read much more was viewed as eccentric – and probably a little unhealthy, too.

We can pick up on this minimalist attitude to reading in early visual depictions of St Jerome, one of the heroes of Christian scholarship. St Jerome was, by all accounts, the supreme intellect of Christendom in the 5th century and beyond; he translated the Greek and Hebrew portions of the Bible into Latin, wrote a large number of commentaries on scripture and is now the patron saint of libraries and librarians. But despite his scholarly efforts, when artists came to depict where and how St Jerome worked, a detail stands out: there are almost no books in his famous study. Strikingly, the most intelligent and thoughtful intellectual of the early Church seems to have read fewer books than an average modern 8-year-old. In this painting by Antonello da Messina, painted just over fifty years after St Jerome's death, the subject appears to be the proud owner of no more than around ten books.

Antonello da Messina, *St Jerome in His Study*, c. 1475

The modern world has dramatically parted ways with this minimalist premodern approach to reading. We have instead adopted an Enlightenment mantra that drives us in the opposite direction. It states that there should be no limit to how much we read, because there is only one answer to the question of *why* we read that can be ambitious enough: we read in order to know everything. We're not reading to understand God or to follow civic virtue or to calm our minds. We are reading to understand the whole of human existence, the full inventory of our trajectory through time, the complete account of all of planetary progress and the entirety of cosmic history. We are collective believers in the idea of totalising knowledge; the more books we have produced and digested, the closer we will be to grasping *everything*.

The sheer scale of this ambition helps to explain why images of libraries in the Enlightenment period depict vast and endless palaces to learning – hinting that perhaps, if money had been no object, these temples to intelligence would have been constructed to ring the Earth.

We may not be aware of how indebted we are to the Enlightenment theory of reading, but its maximalist

Étienne-Louis Boullée, *Restoration of the National Library*, 1785–1788

legacy is present in the publishing industry, in the way books are discussed and written about – and in our own culturally guilty consciences.

We can also hazard an observation: this exhaustive approach to reading does not make us particularly happy. We are drowning in books; we have no time to reread the books we love and we appear condemned to a permanent sense of being under-read compared to our peers and to what the prestigious voices have declared respectable.

In order to ease and simplify our lives, we might dare to ask the same question that St Jerome and his premodern contemporaries considered: *what am I reading for?* And this time, rather than answering, 'In order to know everything,' we might decide on a much more limited, focused and useful goal. We might decide that while society as a whole is on a search for total knowledge, all we really need is to gather the knowledge that is going to be useful to us as we lead our own lives. We might decide on a new mantra to guide our reading henceforth: *I read so I can learn to be content*. Nothing more, nothing less.

With this new, targeted ambition in mind, much of the pressure to read constantly, copiously and randomly starts to fade. Suddenly, like St Jerome, we might have only a dozen books on our shelves – and yet in no way feel intellectually undernourished or deprived.

Once we know that we are reading to be content, we won't need frantically to keep up with every book published each new season. Instead, we can zero in on the titles that best explain what we, personally, deem to be the constituent parts of contentment. For example, we might look for a few key books that explain our psyches to us and that teach us about how families work and how they might work better. One or two that take us through how to find a job we can love and how to build the courage to develop our opportunities, too. We'll probably need some books that discuss friendship and love, sexuality and health. We'll want books about how to travel, how to appreciate, how to be grateful and how to forgive. We can also look for books that help us to stay calm, fight despair and diminish our disappointments. Finally, we'll search out books that gently guide us on how to minimise regret and learn to die well.

With these goals in mind, we won't need a boundless library. The more we understand what reading is for us, the more we can enjoy intimate relationships with just a few important works. Our libraries can be simple. Instead of always broaching new material, we can spend time rereading, paying attention to the reinforcement of what we already know but tend so often to forget. The truly well-read person isn't the one who has read a gargantuan number of books, but someone who has let themselves, and their capacity to live and die well, be profoundly shaped by a very few well-chosen titles.

iii. How to care less about the news

In the modern world, we are under constant pressure to check the news – at times almost minute by minute – and there are vast resources devoted to ensuring we can do so. It feels so completely normal to us that we may sometimes feel compelled to interrupt whatever we are doing (bathing a child or catching up with our grandmother) to learn about the ghastliest and most divisive events that may just have unfolded anywhere in the world.

The earliest kinds of 'news bulletins' were limited to a very select audience. They consisted of the reports of spies and ambassadors, and described events at foreign courts or trends in agriculture or manufacturing. Early 'news' enabled a monarch to quash a revolt, seize an opportunity at sea or strengthen defences against an invasion. Hardly anyone would hear these news bulletins, but the professionals who did so knew exactly what to do with them.

Today, technology and a democratic spirit have enabled the vast, almost universal, distribution of information to pretty much everyone for very little money. Reports that were once intended for a few select ears in government now come to us all. It's flattering, but it can also be confusing, enraging and puzzling. What are we really meant to do with the reams of information we receive? We are left to fret helplessly about what should be done about refugees, the foreign debt, relations with the French, the updating of nuclear reactors and the scandal with the adulterous pop star.

Even when we have no ability to take action of any kind and don't understand the details of what we are being told, updates on national and international problems keep landing on our screens – at the same time that we're trying to take the kids to school or finish some homework, chat to a friend or attempt to lie quietly in the bath. The gift of the news may be flattering; the question is whether much of it is really useful or relevant.

An additional factor that makes our exposure to news more troublesome is that the news is deeply biased towards the most frightening and distressing events. A murder is news, while a young family having a pleasant afternoon with an aunt isn't; we're informed about an outbreak of food poisoning, but not that lots of people's tomato plants are doing nicely this year. The extreme opinions of a small number of highly peculiar people are continuously brought to our attention in a way that average decency rarely is. We therefore come away from every engagement with the news a little more agitated and worried – and a little more convinced of our own powerlessness in the face of a seemingly foolish species.

To construct a wiser relationship to the news and to simplify how much of it we might need, we should focus on a much-neglected but critical question: *what information do we actually require – and what do we actually require it for?* News organisations are deeply resistant to such enquiries and would likely stress that the news is important per se, and that there is no limit to how much of it anyone needs. In a perfect world, we would know everything from everywhere, all at once. But the reality is that the news we really need isn't just any information that has happened to seize the attention of journalists around the world in the last few hours – it is the information that we need in order to flourish as individuals.

The most urgent news we need to hear today might not be about the American government's trade policy announcement, but about our need to control our temper around a sibling who refuses to acknowledge our tortuous past. It might, from a geopolitical perspective, be crucial that the Chinese are intending to make major investments in Kazakhstan today – but it may be much more important for us to think about how little we have recently paid attention to our cousin or the beauty of the evening sky.

The news we see every day is highly restricted in its vision of where to find the crucial facts we need in order to flourish: it sees boardrooms, parliaments, film studios and the luxury homes of celebrities as the primary places to discover what truly matters. We do need to be well informed, of course. But the information that is really relevant to us is likely to be located elsewhere: it may lie in the sceptical look of a 7-year-old who thinks we should play more and work less, in the mood of a few acquaintances in the park, in the thoughts of someone on their deathbed or in the pages of a book written 500 years ago.

Very often, the truly significant news is trapped inside our own mind – but the crush of news from without hampers our ability to pick up on our own tentative thoughts and emerging ideas. The news gives us one of the most prestigious excuses ever invented to never spend time roaming freely inside our own thoughts. Of course, the news that is broadcast to us will be important to someone, somewhere – but most of the time it is wholly disconnected from our own real priorities over the coming years, which are to make the most of our life and our talents in the time that remains to us.

As well as residing inside of us, sometimes the news we need can be very old. Information that is incredibly important for us may well have nothing to do with what's happening in the world right now – but it is still news, because it is information we urgently need to know about in order to flourish. It could be crucial news for us that an Austrian doctor discovered a link between childhood trauma and adult anxiety – even though this development occurred more than a hundred years ago in Sigmund Freud's office in Vienna. Or it might be vital news to learn of an uplifting attitude to art in which works were systematically used to foster spiritual elevation – even though this happened in France in the later 12th century. We might not have got the bulletin about the surprising extent to which we routinely avoid defining what we mean by the keywords we rely on – even though this breakthrough was made by Socrates in ancient Athens around 406 BCE. There's so much 'news' we need to know in order to flourish; so little of it happened in the last few hours.

We can liberate ourselves from our enervating addiction to the news cycle not when we abandon the longing to be well informed, but when we allow ourselves to be more ambitious about what 'well informed' really means. To have a working picture of the wider world may take only a few minutes every day – but to understand what we need to flourish as humans is the work of a lifetime. If the news offered us what we truly needed, it would be worthy of our constant attention. As it is, we can – in good conscience and with great relief – largely ignore it, simplify our days and use our new-found time to roam more imaginatively through the world for the information that will genuinely help us.

iv. How to travel less

At some point in the 1650s, the French philosopher and mathematician Blaise Pascal jotted down one of the most seemingly counterintuitive aphorisms of all time: 'The sole cause of man's unhappiness is that he cannot stay quietly in his room.'

Really? Surely staying quietly in one's room is the beginning of a particularly evolved kind of psychological torture? What could be more opposed to the human spirit than to inhabit just four walls when there is a whole planet to explore?

Pascal's idea challenges one of our most cherished beliefs: that we must always go to new places in order to feel and discover new and worthwhile things. What if, instead, there were already a treasury inside us? What if we had, within our own brains, already accumulated a sufficient number of awe-inspiring, calming and interesting experiences to last us ten lifetimes? What if our real problem is not that we haven't had time to travel enough – but that we don't know how to make the most of what is already to hand?

Restricting ourselves to a simpler life spent at home provides us with a range of curious benefits. The first is an encouragement to think. Whatever we like to believe, few of us do much of the solitary, original, bold kind of thinking that can restore our spirits and move our lives forward. If we were to travel more ambitiously around our minds while lying on the sofa, the new ideas we might stumble upon could threaten our mental status quo – an original thought might, for example, deviate from what the people around us consider normal, and therefore alienate us. Or it might herald a realisation that we've been pursuing the wrong approach to an important issue in our lives, perhaps for a long time. If we were to take one of these new ideas seriously, we might have to abandon a relationship, leave a job, ditch a friend, apologise to someone, rethink our sexuality or break a habit.

However, a period of quiet thinking, alone in our room, provides an occasion for the mind to order and understand itself. Fears, resentments and hopes become easier to name; we grow less scared of the contents of our own minds – and less resentful, calmer and clearer about our direction. We start, in faltering steps, to know ourselves slightly better.

Another thing we can do in our own rooms is to return to journeys we have already taken. This is not a fashionable idea. Most of the time, we are given powerful encouragement to engineer new kinds of travel experiences. The idea of revisiting a journey in memory sounds a little strange – or simply sad. This is an enormous pity. We are careless curators of our own pasts; we push the important scenes from our memories to the back of the cupboard of our minds and don't particularly expect to see them again.

But what if we were to alter the hierarchy of prestige that we have built around travel, and argue that regular immersion in our memories of previously taken trips could be a critical part of what sustains and consoles us – and not least one of the cheapest and most flexible forms of entertainment. It can be almost as interesting to sit at home and reflect on a holiday we once took to an island as it is to trek to the island with our cumbersome bodies.

In our neglect of our memories, we are spoilt children, squeezing only a portion of the pleasure from experiences before tossing them aside to seek new thrills. Part of why we feel the need for so many new experiences may simply be that we are so bad at absorbing the ones we have had.

We do not need a camera or anything technical to help us focus more on the memories we already hold. There is a camera in our minds already: it is always on, taking snapshots of everything we've ever seen. Huge chunks of experience are still there in our heads, intact and vivid, just waiting for us to ask ourselves leading questions like: 'Where did we go after we landed?' or 'What was the first breakfast like?' Our experiences have not disappeared just because they are no longer unfolding right in front of our eyes; we can remain in touch with so much of what made them pleasurable simply through the art of evocation. We talk endlessly of virtual reality, yet we don't need gadgets – we have the finest virtual reality machines already in our own heads. We can – right now – shut our eyes and travel into, and linger among, the very best and most consoling, life-enhancing moments of our pasts.

We travel in the belief that, of course, the reality of a scene must be nicer than the mental image we form of it at home. But there is a curious fact about the way our minds work that we would do well to study when we regret our inability to go anywhere. That is, that there will always be something else on the lens between us and the destination we travel to – something so tricky and oppressive as to somewhat undermine the purpose of having left home in the first place – namely, ourselves. We bring ourselves along to every destination we ever want to enjoy – and that means bringing along the mental baggage that makes being us so intolerably problematic day to day: all the anxiety, regret, confusion, guilt, irritability and despair. None of this smear of the self is there when we picture a trip from home for a few minutes. In the imagination, we can enjoy unsullied views. But when we are really there, at the foot of a golden temple or high up on a pine-covered mountain, we find that there is so much of 'us' intruding on our vista. We ruin our trips through the fateful habit of taking ourselves along on them. There's a tragicomic irony at work, in that the vast labour of getting ourselves physically to a place won't necessarily get us any closer to the essence of what we seek. We should remind ourselves that we may already enjoy the very best that any place has to offer us simply by thinking about it.

Another Frenchman with a comparable underlying philosophy to that of Pascal was the 27-year-old writer Xavier de Maistre. In the spring of 1790, while under house arrest, de Maistre decided to take advantage of this enforced isolation and study the wonders and beauty of what lay closest to him, entitling the account of what he had seen *A Journey Around My Room*.

The book is a charming shaggy dog story – a humorous and long winded yarn, which successfully subverts the travel writing genre. De Maistre locks his door and changes into a pair of pink and blue pyjamas. Without the need for luggage, he 'travels' to the sofa – the largest piece of furniture in the room, which he looks at through fresh eyes and appreciates anew. He admires the elegance of its feet and remembers the pleasant hours he has spent cradled in its cushions, dreaming of love and professional success. From his sofa, de Maistre spies his bed. Once again, from a traveller's vantage point, he learns to appreciate this complex piece of furniture. He feels grateful for the nights he has spent in it and takes pride that his sheets almost match his pyjamas. 'I advise every man who can to get himself pink and white bed linen,' he writes, for these are the colours to induce calm and pleasant reveries in the fragile sleeper.

However playful, de Maistre's work springs from a profound insight: that the pleasure we derive from journeys is perhaps dependent more on the mindset with which we travel than on the destination we travel to. If only we could apply a travelling mindset to our own rooms and immediate neighbourhoods, we might find that these places become no less interesting than foreign lands.

What, then, is a travelling mindset? Receptivity, appreciation and gratitude might be its chief characteristics. And, crucially, this mindset doesn't need to wait for a faraway journey to be deployed.

A walk is the smallest sort of journey we can ever undertake. It stands in relation to a typical holiday as a bonsai tree does to a forest. But even if it is only an eight-minute interlude around the block or a few moments in a nearby park, a walk is already a journey in which many of the grander themes of travel are present.

We might, on such a walk, catch sight of a flower. It is extremely rare to delight in flowers properly when one is young and hopeful – and can at any point take off to another continent. There are so many larger, grander things to be concerned about than these small, delicately sculpted, fragile manifestations of nature. However, it is also rare to be entirely indifferent to flowers after one has lived and suffered a little. Once we have been touched by the sorrows of life, flowers no longer seem like a petty distraction from a mighty destiny; no longer an insult to ambition, but a genuine pleasure amidst a litany of troubles – an invitation to bracket anxieties; a small resting place for hope in a sea of difficulties.

We may also spot a small animal: a duck or a hedgehog. Its life goes on utterly oblivious to ours. It is entirely devoted to its own purposes. The habits of its species have not changed for centuries. We may look at it intently, but it feels not the slightest curiosity about who we are; from its point of view, we are absorbed into the immense blankness of unknowable, incomprehensible things. A duck will take a piece of bread as gladly from a criminal as from a high court judge; from a billionaire as from a bankrupt felon – our individuality is suspended and, on certain days, that can be an enormous relief.

On our walk around the block, themes we've lost touch with – childhood, an odd dream we had recently, a friend we haven't seen for years, a big task we had always told ourselves we'd undertake – float into our attention. In physical terms, we're hardly going any distance at all, but we're crossing acres of mental territory. A short while later, we'll be back at home once again. No one has missed us, or perhaps even noticed that we've been out. Yet we are subtly different: a slightly more complete, more visionary, courageous and imaginative version of the person we knew how to be before we wisely went on a modest journey.

It cannot be a coincidence that many of the world's greatest thinkers have spent unusual amounts of time very simply, alone in their rooms. Silence gives us an opportunity to appreciate a great deal of what we generally see without ever properly noticing, and to understand what we have felt but not yet adequately processed.

When we lead quiet and simple lives, we aren't deprived; we have been granted the privilege of being able to travel the unfamiliar, sometimes daunting, but essentially wondrous continents inside our own minds.

Conclusion

i. How to retire early

One of the most common and deeply cherished fantasies of our times is the idea that we might 'retire early'. Websites promising to help us achieve this dream abound – including managing our finances, working out where we might live and helping us to decide how close we might want to be to the beach – or perhaps a mountain.

What we often miss during these glowing discussions of early retirement, however, is the extraordinary work that is being done by the apparently innocuous term 'retirement'. This word manages to pull off an astonishing feat: it momentarily anaesthetizes all those who hear it into forgetting society's founding pressures and most ingrained competitive values. It renders deeply desirable states of inaction that could otherwise appear simply contemptible or downright lazy.

Someone in the prime of life who loses any interest in going to the office, who doesn't care about promotion and who isn't trying to accumulate ever more money would standardly be described as a loser. Unless, that is, they declare that what they want to do is 'retire early' – at which point they are transformed in our eyes into fascinating and near-saintly figures. We know now that they have stopped working not because they are incompetent or got sacked or are mentally weak-willed. They were almost certainly very good at their jobs; they just gave them up freely to focus their attention on a host of intriguing things that gratify them far more.

Strikingly, at present, we only invoke the idea of retirement in regards to employment. This is a profound pity, because there are so many other things that it might be extremely important for us to stop doing, but which we feel obliged to continue with because we are under punishing pressure from others to conform. 'Retirement' is the word we should learn to use to explain quitting a host of activities otherwise deemed crucial without forfeiting our claim to be classed as honourable and dignified.

Ironically, it might not even be work that many of us most want to retire from. We might be far keener to retire from, let's say, late nights, going to the theatre, using social media, holidaying abroad or having sex with new people. Take the idea of announcing 'early retirement' from parties. Usually, if someone turns down every invitation and stays at home, they'd be seen as lonely and withdrawn – and probably unfit for human company. But suppose we could say that we'd 'retired' from social life; our decision would instantly acquire nobility and prestige. We'd be seen to be giving it up not because we couldn't stand other people or because we were gauche or unpopular; rather the implication would be that we might have been perfectly capable of making witty conversation over cocktails – but that we had decided we'd done enough of that sort of thing and were going to concentrate instead on deepening our friendships with just two or three people or on learning a new language by ourselves in bed.

The same idea holds when considering material competitiveness. We could step back from having an impressive car or a large house and declare that we were 'retiring from consumer society'. While such a move would typically be seen as a mark of failure, with the word 'retirement' now attached to it we can imply that our interests have been willingly and intelligently redirected towards more aesthetic or spiritual targets.

The current notion of retirement is unimaginative about what an individual might retire from. Mostly, the vision is that one stops working so as to be able to undertake outdoor leisure pursuits – tennis, gardening, sailing – and perhaps move to a place with a milder climate. But we can be more ambitious about both what we unshackle ourselves from and what we aspire to do instead: we could retire to connect more deeply with our own minds, to develop our creative potential, to keep a handle on anxiety or to explore who we could be if we stopped caring so much about what other people thought of us.

Reference to retirement also softens the blow for others. When we retire from work, people don't feel we're letting them down – our colleagues will perhaps throw a party for us, congratulate us and say how much they'll miss us. Likewise, by announcing our retirement from social life or relationships, we're making it clear that there's no suppressed personal hatred at play in our decision. We're just rejigging our priorities.

It's ironic that life advice for the young so overwhelmingly focuses on what to do in one's career. In a wiser society, the emphasis would also be on retiring – as early as possible – from a host of supposedly necessary demands that, on closer inspection, are entirely unsuited to who and what we are. Our societies are very keen for us to have busy, competitive, complicated lives. We should express thanks for the well-meaning suggestions and then, as soon as possible and without causing anyone offence, announce our early retirement in the name of the simpler, kinder lives we long for.

ii. Glamour and simplicity

One reason why we often don't dare to adopt the simple life we want is that doing so has rarely been made to seem very glamorous. The perceived glamour of the world is overwhelmingly held to lie in noisy and costly ways of living. We hear about the glamour of owning a large house, of dancing late at night in a crowded bar, of pursuing a career on three continents and of starring in a film or releasing an album.

But very occasionally, and very usefully, talented artists come along and help to reveal the hidden glamour of simple ways of life.

During China's Song dynasty (960–1279), the prominent artist Ma Lin depicted a range of individuals who had retreated to the countryside. One of his major works depicts a scholar, informally dressed, sitting on the bent trunk of an ancient pine tree and listening to the

Ma Lin, *Listening Quietly
to Soughing Pines*, c. 1246

wind. The wind is an elemental force; we hardly pay
attention to the air, but its currents shape our world:

even a gentle breeze will, in time, weather the hardest rock. To listen to the wind means – symbolically – to be attentive to the real, but less obvious, factors that define our true situation.

This image has a specific political context. Instead of pursuing heroic, bustling administrative reforms in the great urban centres, the emerging idea at the time was to undertake gradual, local change in out-of-the-way places. It's a vision of simpler, more modest action – a quiet wind rather than a great storm – that is advanced not as a feeble alternative, but as the wiser and, in the long run, more effective policy.

Towards the end of the 1400s, during the Ming dynasty (1368–1644), the highly successful court artist Zhong Li painted a large silk scroll, nearly two metres tall; it is perhaps his greatest work. It doesn't show the grandeur of the era's military or political achievements. Instead, it presents us with the tiny figure of a reclusive scholar seated on a craggy promontory, contemplating the towering mountains, the mist and a huge waterfall.

At one level it is an immensely sophisticated image: the composition is extremely delicate and refined. But it is presenting us with an idea central to the very notion

Zhong Li, *Scholar Looking at a Waterfall*, 15th century

of simplicity. Symbolically, the water falling into the void and the mountains seemingly rising forever represent the totality of the universe. Contemplating the picture, we merge with the order of the cosmos;

Shen Quan, *Pine, Plum and Cranes*, 1759

our local, immediate concerns drop away. The scholar's situation, alone in the wilds on a foggy day, has nothing in common with what societies have typically seen as a glamorous life. But the artwork gives the scene the honour it deserves: it holds up this solitary, simple state of mind as one of the greatest, most sublime moments of existence, fully deserving of our devotion. Zhong Li glamorises contemplation.

Later, during the Qing dynasty (1644–1912), the painter Shen Quan produced widely acclaimed masterpieces that artfully promote simplicity. In one of his greatest works, *Pine, Plum and Cranes*, he deploys all the appealing resources of composition, colour, brushwork and sensuous beauty to attract us; but the deeper symbolism of the work speaks plainly of a simpler existence.

The gnarled pine tree, rising on the right, represents steadfast endurance; it's not showy – it lives on rugged hillsides and copes well with frost and drought. The tree is a call to us, the viewer, to become more like it: to be less focused on luxury and more interested in independence, even if that means a degree of hardship – which can, as the pine shows, be borne with dignity.

The white plum blossom, in the middle of the scene, is a touching symbol of transience: the plum produces especially delicate, small flowers and they last for only a few days before they fall. The blossom asks us to contemplate the brevity of our own existence, foregrounding a fundamental perspective in which conventional successes and possessions don't look so impressive. It invites us to prioritise what truly matters to us in our all-too-brief sojourn on Earth.

The cranes, or herons, carry dual meaning. They are representations of creatures that have no interest in human affairs – that don't follow the news or fashion and who can't understand our notions of social prestige – but there's an additional layer of symbolic significance, too. In classical Chinese art, herons are seen as long-lived: they represent the accumulation of wisdom. The prestige of art is being used to promote the ideal of a simpler, more focused life.

We are creatures who are, by nature, open to social influence; we take our cues from what surrounds us. Whatever is glamorised becomes easier, and more normal, to love. Ideally, we'd inhabit a world that always supported our best instincts; but, even without public encouragement, we can create this kind of culture – privately, for ourselves – with the help of a few beloved artists.

Kamo no Chōmei glamorised financial modesty; Le Corbusier glamorised small apartments; Picasso glamorised simple drawings; Agnes Martin glamorised restrained mark-making. Not only are we not alone in our search for simplicity, we're endorsed and encouraged by some of the greatest figures of our collective past. In embracing simplicity, we join our lives with theirs; a portion of their glamour becomes ours.

iii. Purpose and simplicity

A key theme that has pursued us throughout this book is that our lives grow more complicated the less we stop to ask what things are for, why we are doing them and how we really feel about them. And, correspondingly, that the more we enquire what possessions, careers, relationships, travels, books and so on are actually doing for us, the more we can decide which of them might be dispensed with and which are worth holding on to. It is secure knowledge of our purpose that is our guide to editing down the complexity of our lives.

Existence becomes overcomplicated when we submit ourselves to tasks or possessions without having a clear sense of their purpose. When we don't properly know why we're doing something, we don't know how much of it we need in our life. Simplicity, therefore, can be defined as the result and precious fruit of clarifying our goals.

Unfortunately, the question of purpose is one that our society at large constantly shies away from. Because of a collective emphasis on freedom and an economic system based on infinite consumer choice, it is made to seem impertinent and unprofitable to demand an explanation as to why we might want to own or read or pursue or do certain things. This is why, ultimately, modern existence feels so complicated. Millions of possibilities are offered to us, but we are never encouraged to stop and ask what any of them might actually be for.

The crucial step towards leading a simpler life isn't – as we might initially suppose – to get rid of things. It's to ask ourselves what our true longings are and what are the ends at which we are aiming. Simplicity isn't so much a life with few things and commitments in it, as a life with the right, necessary things, attuned to our flourishing. Our lives will feel – and be – simpler when we've probed our minds to yield up their most secret and precious insight: the knowledge of what we truly want.

Image credits

Cover   Wittgenstein Stiftelsen Skjolden / Wittgenstein Initiative Vienna

p. 9   Courtesy of Rockefeller Archive Center. https://rockarch.org/

p. 9   Courtesy of Rockefeller Archive Center https://rockarch.org/

p. 10   Vespasian / Alamy Stock Photo

p. 11   Attributed to Antonio Rodriguez, *Portrait of Moctezuma*,
          c. 1680. Oil on canvas, 182 cm × 106.5 cm. Tesoro dei Granduchi,
          Florence, Italy / Wikimedia Commons

p. 12   Justin Sullivan / Getty Images

p. 13   *The Sitting Woman* and *The Thinker*, Hamangia culture, Romania,
          5200–4500 BCE. National History and Archaeology Museum,
          Constanta, Romania. DEA / G. DAGLI ORTI /
          De Agostini / Getty Images

p. 14   Michelangelo, terracotta modello for the Pietà, c. 1473–1496.
          Private Collection.

p. 15   Henry Moore, *Reclining Woman*, 1930. Sculpture in green
          Hornton stone, 41.3 cm × 94 cm × 59.7 cm. Reproduced by
          permission of The Henry Moore Foundation © The Henry Moore
          Foundation. All Rights Reserved, DACS / www.henry-moore.org

p. 17   Élisabeth Louise Vigée Le Brun, *Marie Antoinette in Court Dress*,
          1778. Oil on canvas, 273 cm × 193.5 cm. Kunsthistorisches
          Museum, Vienna, Austria / Wikimedia Commons

p. 18   Pictorial Press Ltd / Alamy Stock Photo

p. 121 The Ife Head, Yoruba culture, c. 14th–15th century. Brass, 35 cm × 12.5 cm × 15 cm. The British Museum, London, England. Registration number: Af1939,34.1. sailko / Wikimedia Commons (CC BY-SA 3.0)

p. 124 Geffrye Museum / Alamy Stock Photo

p. 125 Peter Cook-VIEW / Alamy Stock Photo

p. 126 Douglas Kirkland / Getty Images

p. 127 Tea bowl, White Satsuma ware, 17th century. Stoneware with clear, crackled glaze, stained by ink; gold lacquer repairs, 10.5 cm × 12.2 cm. Freer Gallery of Art, Smithsonian Institution, Washington, D.C. Gift of Charles Lang Freer, F1904.323

p. 128 Oleksiy Maksymenko Photography / Alamy Stock Photo

p. 129 © John Pawson

p. 130 New Africa / Shutterstock

p. 131 Elizabeth Whiting & Associates / Alamy Stock Photo

p. 145 Alexandre Cabanel, *Cincinnatus receiving the ambassadors of Rome*, 1843. Oil on canvas, 114 cm × 146 cm. Fabre Museum, Montpellier, France / Wikimedia Commons

p. 148 Agnes Martin, *Affection*, 2001. Acrylic and graphite on canvas, 152.4 cm x 152.4 cm. © Agnes Martin Foundation, New York / DACS 2021

p. 167 Antonello da Messina, *St Jerome in his study*, c. 1475. Oil on lime, 45.7 cm × 36.2 cm. National Gallery, London, England / Wikimedia Commons

p. 169 Étienne-Louis Boullée, *Restoration of the National Library*,
1785–1788. Wash and black ink on paper, 98 cm × 63 cm.
National Library of France, Paris, France / Wikimedia Commons

p. 197 Ma Lin, *Listening Quietly to Soughing Pines*, c. 1246. Hanging
Scroll, Colour on silk, 226.6 cm × 110.3 cm. National Palace
Museum, Taibei, Taiwan / Wikimedia Commons

p. 199 Zhong Li, *Scholar Looking at a Waterfall*, 15th century. Hanging
scroll; ink and color on silk, 318.8 cm × 126 cm. The Metropolitan
Museum of Art, New York, USA. From the P. Y. and Kinmay W. Tang
Family Collection, Gift of Oscar L. Tang, 1991.

p. 200 Shen Quan, *Pine, Plum and Cranes*, 1759. Hanging scroll,
ink and colour on silk, 191 cm × 98.3 cm. Palace Museum, Beijing,
China / Wikimedia Commons

The School of Life is a global organisation helping people lead more fulfilled lives. It is a resource for helping us understand ourselves, for improving our relationships, our careers and our social lives – as well as for helping us find calm and get more out of our leisure hours. We do this through films, workshops, books, apps, gifts and community. You can find us online, in stores and in welcoming spaces around the globe.

THESCHOOLOFLIFE.COM